POCKET
FOOTBALL
STARS

Published in June 2020

A catalogue record for this book is available from the British Library

ISBN 978 1 78521 729 6

Library of Congress control no. 2019956351

Design and layout by Richard Parsons

Published by Haynes Publishing,
Sparkford, Yeovil, Somerset BA22 7JJ, UK
Tel: 01963 440635, Int. tel: +44 1963 440635
Website: www.haynes.com

Haynes North America Inc.,
859 Lawrence Drive, Newbury Park, California 91320, USA

Printed in China

The Author

This is the sixth football pocket manual Nick has written for Haynes. He's been
editing football publications for more than 20 years and continues to follow Swindon
Town Football Club. The Robins' striker, Eoin Doyle, enjoyed a better record in front
of goal than many strikers included in this book, even if it was in League Two.

POCKET MANUAL
FOOTBALL STARS

FOOTBALL STARS
CONTENTS

30 UNDER 30   110

Keep your eyes on these
bright young internationals
in 2020 and beyond.

FANTASY XI   126

Time to take on the role as
manager and pick a starting XI
from our top 50!

FOOTBALL STARS
A-Z OF FOOTBALL

Think you know your football? You will if you follow our handy alphabetical guide to some of the words and phrases used in the sport.

Association football

Football. Footie. Soccer. Fitbar. Calcio. Fútbol … whatever you call it, the earliest form of 'the beautiful game' is believed to have been a competitive version called *Cuju*, which originated in China between 206BC and AD220. The modern rules originated in the 1800s in England. They were an attempt to standardise the various forms of the games played in public schools around the country.

Back-pass rule

The back-pass rule prevents goalkeepers from handling the ball after it has been deliberately passed back to them, or thrown to them from a throw-in, by a teammate. The rule was introduced in 1992 in an attempt to stop time wasting and negative or over-defensive play, and it was first introduced at the Olympic Games that year.

Clean sheet

The holy grail for a goalkeeper is a 'clean sheet'. This is when they prevent the opposition from scoring a goal in a match. The record for the most clean sheets in the Premier League is 202, held by former Arsenal and Chelsea goalkeeper Petr Čech. The Czech legend also holds the record for the most clean sheets in a single season: 24. With 102 shut outs, goalkeeping legends Iker Casillas (Spain) and Hope Solo (USA) boast the most clean sheets at international level.

Derby

A derby match is a game between two teams located geographically close (same city or nearby cities/countries) or that share a rivalry based on history and/or previous encounters. Notable derbies include Liverpool v Manchester United, Red Star Belgrade v Partizan Belgrade in Serbia, Boca Juniors and River Plate in Argentina, and Barcelona v Real Madrid in Spain.

Extra time

Extra time usually consists of two halves of 15 minutes and is used in cup matches to determine which team wins, when the scores have been level after 90 minutes, otherwise known as 'normal time'.

Football acronyms

EFL:	English Football League
FA:	Football Association
FIFA:	Fédération Internationale de Football Association (International Federation of Football Association)
MVP:	Most Valuable Player
NCAA:	National Collegiate Athletic Association (USA)
FA WSL:	(or WSL), Football Association Women's Super League
PFA:	Professional Football Association
UEFA:	Union of European Football Association

Formation

The way in which the players in a team position themselves on the pitch depends on their formation is part of the team's 'tactics'; i.e. how they plan to win a game. Popular formations include the 4-3-2-1, otherwise known as the 'Christmas Tree', plus 4-4-2, 4-5-1, or 4-3-3. The first number relates to the number of defenders, the middle number/s to the midfielders and the last to the attackers. Formations can be defensive or attacking, narrow or wide. They can also be interchangeable, or 'fluid'.

Giant-killing

A giant-killing can also be referred to as a 'cup upset' or 'shock' and involves an underdog (see U) beating a favourite, a David beating a Goliath … basically a team beating another team that is ranked significantly higher than them. A good example of this was in the FA Cup in 2015, when Bradford City, then in League One (England's third tier) came from two goals behind to beat Premier League giants Chelsea, who were 49 places above their opponents.

Hospital ball

Receive one of these and you could be in trouble! It describes a pass that leaves the recipient open to heavy contact from an opposing player. It's usually avoidable, and the term itself implies that the recipient could end up in hospital.

International

The best players earn call-ups for their representative national teams. Every four years, the best of these representative teams compete against each other in an attempt to win the World Cup. Historically, the most successful nation is Brazil, who have won the World Cup five times. Each continent also hosts its own tournament. In Europe, for example, nations compete for the European Championship every four years.

Journeyman

A footballer who plays for numerous clubs during their career is described as a 'journeyman'. A prime example is retired goalkeeper Lutz Pfannenstiel, who played for 27 clubs and is the only player to have played professionally in all six FIFA confederations. Jefferson Louis, who played in England in the 1990s, represented 34 clubs in total!

Kick-off

A game is started or restarted – either at half time, during extra time or after a goal – by one team 'kicking off'. There is a pre-game coin toss to decide who takes the kick-off, and which end of the stadium they'll attack or defend.

Lost the dressing room

A term that refers to when the players of a team no longer respect a manager or follow his instructions. This often leads to said manager being sacked.

Magic sponge

A sponge filled with water that has seemingly magical reviving properties for injured players.

Nutmeg

A skill that involves a player kicking a ball through an opponent's legs to get past them. Luis Suárez, Dele Alli and Tobin Heath are an example of players who love to use a nutmeg to their advantage in the men's and women's games respectively.

Offside

Always tricky to explain without using visual aids, the offside rule states that a player is judged to be offside when any body part in the opponents' half of the pitch is closer to the opponents' goal line than both the ball and the second-last opponent. To be judged offside, a player must be involved in 'active play'.

Panenka

A technique used by some when taking a penalty kick. Instead of kicking the ball to the left or right of the goalkeeper and with power, a Panenka sees the attacker apply a deft 'dink' to chip the ball towards the centre of the goal. The technique was first used by Czech international Antonín Panenka in the European Championship final in 1976.

Qatar

The controversial destination of the next World Cup in 2022. It will be the first time the tournament will be held in November and December (as opposed to May, June or July).

Register an assist

To provide the final ball that helps another teammate score a goal.

Route one

A generalised term for a direct attack that starts with a long and/or high ball played from defence to attack.

Six pointer

A term used to describe a game between two teams in similar league positions. The winner is awarded three points, but the term is used to describe the context of the match, so not just the value of the three points won by the victor, but also the three points lost by the defeated team.

Transfer window

This is a period during the year in which football clubs can buy or sell players. The transfer window changes from country to country. In England, for example, teams are only allowed to sign or sell players between 17 May and, from next season, the end of August, and 1 January and 31 January.

Underdog

A team that is expected to lose a game because they're not as good as the opposition is generally known as the 'underdog' in any sport. The term originated in the 19th century and came from dog fighting.

Video Assistant Referee

A controversial system introduced in English football in 2019, a team of officials stationed inside a video-operating room – reviews decisions made by the match referee in an attempt to correct clear and obvious errors and serious missed incidents.

These include whether or not a goal should be given, whether or not a penalty should be awarded, if a player should be given a straight red card, and to ensure the correct player is awarded a red or yellow card.

War chest

When a manager is given a sum of money to acquire new players in a transfer window (see T), the figure they have to spend is described as a 'war chest'.

X-rated

Malicious or 'dirty' tackles are said to be 'X-rated'. They can be 'clumsy' and/or 'late', but generally result in a player injuring an opponent.

'You don't know what you're doing'

This chant can be applied to match officials or managers whom fans feel have made a mistake or a series of errors. When directed at managers, it's usually followed by: 'You're getting sacked in the morning'.

Row Z

This term refers to a row of seats furthest from the pitch, and is often used to describe how high or wide an attacker has missed the goal by, or where a defender should aim for when clearing the ball or 'getting rid'.

SERGIO AGÜERO

Just when you think Sergio 'Kun' Agüero has peaked, the ruthless Argentine takes his game to another level. This is, of course, great news for Manchester City but less so for Agüero's attacking teammate and Brazilian international Gabriel Jesus, who continues to wait patiently for a regular run in the side. Agüero scored 21 goals in 2018/19 and then, by mid-January in 2020, he'd rattled home 18 goals in 21 starts in all competitions, 13 of which came in the league, which saw him overtake Thierry Henry as the Premier League's most prolific foreign striker ever. It's his most deadly ratio since joining the club in 2011, and puts him on track to beat his highest overall haul of 33 goals in 2016/17.

'This kind of player ... there are not many in the incredible history of English football. He helps to make the Premier League better.'

Manchester City coach Pep Guardiola

HIGHLIGHTS

2003
Agüero makes his debut for Argentine club Independiente aged just 15 years and 35 days, breaking the record previously set by legend Diego Maradona.

2006
He joins Atlético Madrid for €23m. Two years later, he wins an Olympic gold medal with Argentina in Beijing, scoring in the semi-final against Brazil.

2010
Agüero wins both the UEFA Europa League and UEFA Super Cup with Atlético. A year later he joins Manchester City for £35m.

2014
The striker plays with Argentina in the World Cup final in Rio but ends up on the losing side against Germany.

10

FACT FILE

DOB: 02.06.88

HEIGHT: 1.70m (5'7")

WEIGHT: 77kg (170lb)

ARGENTINA: Caps 97 Goals 41

POSITION: Forward

CLUBS: Manchester City (current), Independiente, Atlético Madrid

2016
Agüero ends the 2015/16 campaign with the highest goals-per-minute ratio in the Premier League, averaging a goal every 102 minutes.

2017
With a goal against Napoli, his 178th for Manchester City overall, Agüero overtakes club legend Eric Brook to become City's all-time highest goalscorer.

2019
Agüero scores 21 league goals and wins his fourth Premier League winners' medal. He then adds an FA Cup winners' medal to his collection.

FAMOUS FOR...
Manchester City's highest-ever scorer, Agüero will forever be remembered for the dramatic late goal against QPR in 2012 that secured City's first league title in 44 years.

TRENT
ALEXANDER-ARNOLD

Aged just 21, Liverpool-born Trent Alexander-Arnold is considered by many to be the best attacking right-back in world football. Like teammate Andy Robertson, Alexander-Arnold's game has been catapulted into another stratosphere in the last two years. He ended the 2018/19 season with six assists in six league games, 12 assists in all competitions. He also won a Champions League winners' medal, his appearance against Tottenham Hotspur in Madrid in the final making him the youngest player to start two consecutive Champions League finals. He then clocked his 100th appearance for his boyhood club before Christmas in the 2019/20 season as Liverpool chased a first Premier League title win in 30 years.

> *'I have known Trent Alexander-Arnold since he was 17 years old. He was a big talent, but we were not sure he could do it physically. Now he is a machine.'*
>
> **Liverpool boss Jürgen Klopp**

HIGHLIGHTS

2004
Alexander-Arnold's name is drawn out of a hat, with the prize the chance to attend a half-term camp at Liverpool. It's here that his remarkable journey at the club begins.

2015
He makes his unofficial senior debut in a pre-season friendly against Swindon Town.

2016
The right-back makes his first professional start in the EFL Cup in October and a Premier League debut follows in December.

2017
Named Liverpool's Young Player of the Season. At the start of the following season he scores his first goal, and in doing so becomes the third youngster player to score for Liverpool on his European debut.

FACT FILE

DOB: 07.10.98

HEIGHT: 1.75m (5'9")

WEIGHT: 69kg (152lb)

ENGLAND: Caps **9**
Goals **1**

POSITION: Defender

CLUBS: Liverpool
(current)

2018
Named Liverpool's best young player for the second consecutive season shortly after having become Liverpool's youngest ever player to feature in a Champions League final.

2018
At the World Cup in Russia, Alexander-Arnold becomes only the fourth teenager to feature for England in the competition.

2019
Alexander-Arnold finishes the season with the most assists made by a defender in a single season. He's nominated for the Ballon d'Or award and is voted the 19th best player in the world.

FAMOUS FOR...
Alexander-Arnold's quick thinking from a corner against Barcelona was one of the footballing moments of 2019. His set piece was converted by teammate Divock Origi to seal Liverpool's famous win.

ALISSON
BECKER

Sometimes a player comes along and changes the course of a club's history for the better, and Liverpool struck gold twice in the space of a year when they signed defender Virgil van Dijk in December 2017 and goalkeeper Alisson Becker

'This guy is a phenomenon. He is the Number One of Number Ones. He is the Messi of goalkeepers, because he has the same mentality as Messi.'

Former Roma coach Roberto Negrisolo

the following summer. Becker isn't just ridiculously hard to score against, he also makes important and match-winning saves at vital moments. He is calm, excellent with the ball at his feet, and commands his area at crosses. He also dominates one-on-one situations ... you get the picture. He's the complete goalkeeper who's performing at the highest level on a consistent basis, which is why he was awarded the inaugural Yashin Trophy as the world's best goalkeeper at the Ballon d'Or awards in 2019.

HIGHLIGHTS

2002
A 10-year-old Becker joins Internacional's academy. He rises through the ranks to the first team, where he goes on to make more than 100 appearances.

2013
Makes his league debut in the Campeonato Brasileiro Série in August 2013. Internacional win the league title in each of his four seasons in the first-team squad.

2016
Joins Italian side Roma on a five-year deal. He makes his debut for the 'Giallorossi' in August.

2018
Becker ends the 2017/18 Série A season with 22 clean sheets and Goalkeeper of the Year award, before joining Liverpool for £66.8m. At that time, for four weeks, he was the most expensive goalkeeper in the world.

FACT FILE

DOB: 02.10.92

HEIGHT: 1.90m (6'3")

WEIGHT: 91kg (201lb)

BRAZIL: Caps **44** Goals **0**

POSITION: **Goalkeeper**

CLUBS: Liverpool (current), Internacional, Roma

2018
Makes his senior international debut in October, for Brazil, against Venezuala. Remarkably, he has played a further 43 games since then.

2019
Finishes the 2018/19 campaign with 21 clean sheets, a Champions League winners' medal, and winner of the Golden Glove award.

2019
Becker also wins the 2019 Copa América with Brazil after conceding just one goal in the tournament (six matches).

FAMOUS FOR...
His late point-blank save against Napoli in Liverpool's win-or-bust Champions League match in December 2018 set the Reds on their way to lifting the trophy in May.

KARIM
BENZEMA

Just when you thought the Frenchman might be passing his prime, he goes on a scoring spree that shows little sign of slowing. Since former Real Madrid teammate Cristiano Ronaldo left the club to join Juventus in 2018, Benzema has revelled in the freedom and responsibility of being the main frontman. In fact, he's enjoyed it so much he scored more goals for Madrid (52) in all club matches since Ronaldo left than Ronaldo had netted in Turin (46) by mid-January 2020. Benzema ended the 2018/19 season with eight goals in his last eight games and after scoring four in pre-season, he started the 2019/20 campaign with five in five. He then kicked into 2020 with another seven in nine.

'The best No. 9 in the world and on top of that he makes the other players around him better too.'

Real Madrid teammate Eden Hazard

HIGHLIGHTS

2004
After joining Lyon's academy, and scoring 38 goals in one season, Benzema gets called up to the reserve team, then the senior team by then coach Paul Le Guen. He made his debut in January 2005, against Metz.

2006
Benzema scored his first goals for Lyon in 2005, but his first league goal came in March, against Ajaccio.

2008
The goals start to flow. At the end of the 2007/08 season, Benzema scores 31 goals in 51 games, 20 of which came in the league and saw him top the division's scoring charts. He was named Ligue 1 Player of the Year.

2009
Benzema joins Real Madrid and after scoring five goals in pre-season he nets his first goal in a 5–0 win against Xerez in September. He scores 26 goals in his second season.

FACT FILE

DOB: 19.12.87

HEIGHT: 1.85m (6'1")

WEIGHT: 81kg (179lb)

FRANCE: Caps **81** Goals **27**

POSITION: Forward

CLUBS: Real Madrid (current), Lyon

2012
In March, Benzema overtakes Zinedine Zidane to become the top French scorer in La Liga history. His goals help 'Los Blancos' win a first league title in four years. Two years later he scores his 100th goal for the club.

2017
Overtakes Thierry Henry in the list of all-time Champions League goalscorers. Madrid win a league and Champions League double. A year later, Madrid win their third consecutive Champions League title.

2018
Benzema nets his 200th goal for Madrid, becoming only the seventh player to do so. He also becomes only the second player behind Lionel Messi to score in 15 consecutive seasons.

DID YOU KNOW?
Benzema is one of only four players – alongside Cristiano Ronaldo, Lionel Messi and Raúl – to score 60 or more goals in the Champions League.

LUCY
BRONZE

English women's football and the England women's national team are on the rise, and that's down to the quality of players such as Lucy Bronze. In 2019, Bronze became the first English player to win the UEFA Women's Player of the Year award after a panel of judges scored her ahead of club teammates Ada Hegerberg and Amandine Henry. And for good reason; Bronze excelled for club and country, her powerful attacking runs and positional awareness making her arguably the best women's right-back in the world. A two-time Champions League winner, Bronze is also a menace in and around opposing areas thanks to her power, pace, shooting and decisive final balls.

> *'The way she takes games by the scruff of the neck, her energy – physically nobody can ever match her; that's in the world probably, never mind Europe.'*
> England teammate Steph Houghton

HIGHLIGHTS

2007
Bronze joins Sunderland's senior team after entering the club's academy at U12 level, and captaining the U16s. At the end of her first season, she wins the Manager's Player of the Year award.

2008
Bronze moves to America to study at the University of North Carolina. In 2009, she becomes the first British player to win a National Collegiate Athletic Association (NCAA) Cup.

2010
Bronze joins Everton. Two years later, she signs for local rivals Liverpool and wins consecutive FA WSL titles in 2013 and 2014.

2014
Bronze is awarded the PFA's Women's Players' Player of the Year award before joining Manchester City.

FACT FILE

DOB: 28.10.91

HEIGHT: 1.73m (5'8")

WEIGHT: 65kg (143lb)

ENGLAND: Caps **79**
Goals **8**

POSITION: Defender

CLUBS: Olympique Lyonnais (current), Sunderland, Everton, Liverpool, Manchester City

2017
Bronze joins French side Olympique Lyonnais, but not before ending the 2016/17 campaign unbeaten with Manchester City, and with an FA WSL Cup winners' medal

2018
In her first season in France, Bronze makes 19 appearances as Lyon win a 12th straight league title. She also scores twice in eight games as they win the Women's Champions League.

2019
Bronze wins a league, Champions League and Coupe de France Féminine treble before helping England reach the World Cup semi-finals.

DID YOU KNOW?
Bronze's second middle name is 'Tough'. Tough by name, tough by nature, never has a name embodied a person so perfectly.

19

KEVIN
DE BRUYNE

A creative mastermind with magic in his boots, Belgian star Kevin De Bruyne is a hugely influential player for club and country. He's so effective it seems he's one step ahead of everyone else on the pitch. A regular goalscorer from midfield, the Belgian exploits opposing areas by running at defenders and delivering laser-accurate passes through the lines or from wide areas. The best example of his brilliance was a mind-bending pass to Leroy Sané in a 7–2 win against Stoke City in October 2017. After receiving the ball from Sané, De Bruyne shaped to shoot but then delivered a 'no-look' pass to take out five Stoke defenders. The move was the highlight of his best season in England; he contributed 21 assists as Manchester City won the league in record-breaking fashion.

'He's a special player. He sees things others cannot see on the pitch, or even off the pitch. He is incredibly talented.'

Manchester City manager Pep Guardiola

HIGHLIGHTS

2005
De Bruyne joins Belgian side Genk after spells at Gent and KVE Drongen. He makes his first-team debut in a 3–0 defeat against Charleroi.

2011
Finishes the 2010/11 season with five goals and 16 assists in 32 league matches as Genk win the Belgian First Division A for the third time in their history.

2012
Moves to Chelsea for £7m in January and makes his debut in pre-season that summer before joining Werder Bremen on loan, where he stars.

2014
Leaves Chelsea for VfL Wolfsburg on a permanent basis, where he wins two cups in one-and-a-half seasons before joining Manchester City.

FACT FILE

DOB: 28.06.91

HEIGHT: 1.80m (5'11")

WEIGHT: 68kg (150lb)

BELGIUM: Caps 74 Goals 19

POSITION: Midfield

CLUBS: Manchester City (current), Genk, Chelsea, Werder Bremen (loan), VfL Wolfsburg

2015
Joins the Citizens for a club record fee of £55m, which makes him the second most expensive player in British football history behind Ángel Di María.

2018
Stars as Belgium reach the World Cup semi-finals. De Bruyne scores one goal and adds one assist.

2019
De Bruyne ends the 2018/19 season with a Premier League winners' medal, and an FA Cup and EFL Cup double. He starts the 2019/20 season by helping City win the Community Shield.

FAMOUS FOR...
De Bruyne contributed his 15th assist of the 2019/20 season in January, making him the first player to make 15 or more assists in three different seasons.

DEBINHA

Brazil goal-scoring legends Marta or Cristiane might be more obvious entries here, given that the former is the greatest player of all time and the latter has a ridiculous goalscoring record. Débora Cristiane de Oliveira, known as Debinha, however, is peaking, and since the World Cup in 2019 the attacking midfielder has been unstoppable; adding clinical finishing and unpredictable creativity to her ability to dominate her opponents. She ended the 2019 WSL season with nine goals and seven assists in 18 starts, including goals in the play-off semi-finals and final to help North Carolina Courage win a second consecutive league title, and scoring five goals in four Brazil internationals.

> *'You never know what she's going to do, and I think that's what makes her so dangerous. We're thankful that we have her on our team. It's just a joy to play with her, honestly.'*
>
> Courage teammate Jaelene Hinkle

HIGHLIGHTS

2011
At the Pan American Games in Guadalajara, Debinha makes her senior international debut. She scores two goals in the tournament, against Costa Rica and Canada.

2012
While at Centro Olímpico, her fifth club, Debinha is a runner-up in the Copa do Brasil. She spends two seasons at the club.

2014
After signing for Norwegian side Avaldsnes, Debinha finishes as the top scorer of the Toppserien, the Norwegian top flight, on 20 goals, four ahead of her nearest rival.

2014
She then goes on loan to Brazil club São José where they win the Copa Libertadores Femenina and the International Women's Club Championship.

FACT FILE

DOB: 20.10.91

HEIGHT: 1.57m (5'2")

WEIGHT: 52kg (115lb)

BRAZIL: Caps 91 Goals 32

POSITION: Attacking midfielder

CLUBS: North Carolina Courage (current), Lorena, Saad Esporte Clube, Portuguesa, Foz Cataratas, Centro Olímpico, Avaldsnes, São José, Dalian Quanjian

2017
Joins North Carolina Courage and scores the club's first goal in their new home stadium. She finishes the season with four goals and after having played every game, she gets injured in the play-off semi-finals.

2018
She scores eight goals in the regular season as Courage win their second straight NWSL shield, and then scores in another final as they win the Championship. Brazil win the Copa America Femenina.

2019
She ends the year with five goals in four internationals, including two against England in a friendly at Middlesbrough's Riverside Stadium.

DID YOU KNOW?
In April 2019, Debinha made history by scoring North Carolina Courage's 100th goal in the National Women's Soccer League (NWSL), against Houston.

23

CRYSTAL
DUNN

In 2015, rising star Crystal Dunn watched USA lift the World Cup in Canada in a bar in Washington, just weeks after she'd been left out of the final squad. Four years later, she made amends for that disappointment, her pace and energy helping the Stars and Stripes retain the title in France. That initial setback in 2015 acted as a huge inspiration for Dunn. In the following domestic season, she scored 15 goals in 20 matches for Washington Spirit and she won the league's Most Valuable Player (MVP) and Golden Boot awards. She returned to USA after a stint at Chelsea to star for North Carolina Courage as they outscored everyone to win the league in 2018. At the World Cup in 2019, Dunn starred from left-back.

'She's the most versatile player I've ever coached. It's not just her ability to play in different lines, it's the quality with which she plays in different lines, which is quite extraordinary.'

Jill Ellis, former USWT national coach

HIGHLIGHTS

2006–2009
Dunn racks up the silverware as she stars for South Side High School, winning three New York state championships and more personal awards than can be listed on this page.

2010–2013
At the University of North Carolina, Dunn adds a long list of personal honours to the NCAA Women's Soccer Championship win in 2012. She makes her international debut, against Scotland, in February 2013.

2014
Joins Washington Spirit and starts 19 of 22 appearances in her first season.

2015
Dunn scores 15 goals to win the NWSL Golden Boot and MVP awards. Aged 23, she becomes the youngest player to do so.

FACT FILE

DOB: 03.07.92

HEIGHT: 1.55m (5'1")

WEIGHT: 54kg (119lb)

USA: Caps **96** Goals **24**

POSITION: Wing-back

CLUBS: North Carolina Courage (current), Washington Spirit, Chelsea

2016
Scores five goals in one game for USA, against Puerto Rico. She also provides an assist. A year later, she joins Chelsea, for whom she scores just 12 minutes into her competitive debut.

2018
Joins North Carolina Courage who break the record for most goals scored in a season and win the NWSL Championship.

2019
Starts 11 games (at the time of writing) and contributes seven goals and adding four assists. She also stars as USA win the World Cup.

DID YOU KNOW?
Dunn's hero is tennis ace Serena Williams, and she once wore the player's name on the back of her shirt as a sign of how much Williams' exploits had inspired her.

EDERSON

A player of futsal, and a left-back in his formative years, goalkeeper Ederson Santana de Moraes, known as Ederson, still loves to play out on pitch in training if the opportunity arises. This matters, because while his shot-stopping abilities are world class, what really sets him apart is his positional play behind the defence and his laser-accurate passing. Ederson is a classic 'goleiro-linha', a goalkeeper who plays with his feet. He uses this to turn defence into attack at lightning speed, to the extent that he's registered more assists than some midfielders. Few Manchester City fans knew much about the Brazilian when Pep Guardiola signed him in 2017 but he has been perfect for Guardiola's style and philosophy, and a pivotal part of City's success under the Spaniard, winning eight trophies.

> *'He's the calmest keeper I've seen. It's like having Ronald Koeman in goal, he gets [the ball] and spins it around the pitch, all over the place.'*
> Burnley manager Sean Dyche

HIGHLIGHTS

2008
Ederson joins local club São Paulo and plays there for one season before moving to Benfica.

2011
Ederson leaves the Portuguese giants after two seasons to join Ribeirão, then Rio Ave a year later.

2015
Ederson rejoins Benfica and in March 2016 he seizes his chance in the first XI, replacing the injured Júlio César and impressing as Benfica win a Primera Liga, Taça de Portugal and Supertaça Cândido de Oliveira treble.

2017
Ederson wins another league and cup double before becoming the second most expensive goalkeeper of all time – now the fourth – when joining Manchester City for £35m. He then makes his debut for Brazil.

FACT FILE

DOB: **17.08.93**

HEIGHT: **1.88m (6'2")**

WEIGHT: **89kg (196lb)**

BRAZIL: Caps **9** Goals **0**

POSITION: **Goalkeeper**

CLUBS: Manchester City (current), Ribeirão, Rio Ave, Benfica B, Benfica

2018

Ederson becomes the first City goalkeeper to register an assist. He wins a league and EFL Cup double at the end of his first season.

2019

After winning three trophies, he wins the Community Shield before adding another league title, plus the FA Cup and EFL Cup at the end of his second season.

DID YOU KNOW?

In October 2018, Ederson broke the Guinness World Record for longest drop kick, registering 75.35m (247'2"). The previous record was 75m (246').

CHRISTIANE
ENDLER

If there were any doubt over the identity of the best women's goalkeeper in the world, Christiane Endler's performances at the 2019 World Cup settled the debate. Endler captained a Chile side playing at the tournament for the first time in their history, and though they lost the opening two games, Endler's performances were among the highlights of the whole competition. She managed to keep Sweden at bay for 83 minutes in the first match, and better followed in match two, when the Paris Saint-Germain keeper faced a USA side who had already put 13 goals past Thailand. Endler made six incredible saves – one stop in particular defying gravity, as she dived to her right to keep out a Christen Press header from point-blank range – and was voted player of the match.

> '**World-class goalkeeper. One of the best shot-stoppers I've ever seen.**'
>
> Former USA coach Jill Ellis

HIGHLIGHTS

2008
Endler enjoys her first taste of World Cup football for Chile's U20s side on home soil and is voted Chilean Female Player of the Year for her performances, an award she wins three times in a row.

2009
Endler wins her first cap for the senior team, against Mexico in November, when she is 18.

2012
Endler attends the University of South Florida and plays in goal for the university team for two years. The same year, she wins a Copa Libertadores winners' medal with Colo-Colo.

2014
Endler joins Chelsea in England, but her time in London is frustrated by injury.

FACT FILE

DOB: 23.07.91

HEIGHT: 1.80m (5'11")

WEIGHT: 65kg (143lb)

CHILE: Caps 69 Goals 0

POSITION: Goalkeeper

CLUBS: Paris Saint-Germain (current), Unión La Calera, Everton, Colo-Colo, Chelsea, Valencia

2015
Endler goes back to Chile to play for Colo-Colo before again returning to Europe, this time to play for Valencia in Spain.

2017
Endler wins an award for conceding the fewest goals in the Spanish league before leaving to sign a three-year contract with French side Paris Saint-Germain.

2019
Endler becomes the first woman to captain Chile at a World Cup and, alongside her teammates, inspires thousands of women in the country to take an interest in football.

DID YOU KNOW?
Endler was 17 when she represented Chile's U20s, who made history by entering their first World Cup competition, the U20s World Cup in 2008, which was held on home soil.

JULIE
ERTZ

US teammate Megan Rapinoe earned the headlines and prizes for her role in USA's World Cup win in 2019, but holding midfielder Julie Ertz continues to be arguably the biggest presence for the Stars and Stripes. A model of consistency ever since she made the transition from USA's U20s to the senior team in 2013, and from centre-back to central holding midfielder, Ertz's career took off when she was drafted by the Chicago Red Stars in 2014. She scored on her National Women's Soccer League (NWSL) debut and ended her first season as Rookie of the Year. In 2015, she became a World Cup winner – the second youngest on the USA team – after playing in every game. She was named in the team of the tournament. In 2017, Ertz was crowned US Soccer Female Player of the Year. She won it again in 2019.

'Julie is incredibly intelligent about the game. She's like having another coach on the field.'
Chicago head coach Rory Dames

HIGHLIGHTS

2010
Ertz is named West Coast Conference Freshman of the Year following an impressive first season with with the Broncos, Santa Clara University's football team.

2012
After a successful junior year at SCU, she's named US Soccer Young Female Athlete of the Year.

2013
Ertz makes her international debut in a 4–1 win against Scotland.

2014
She's the third selection of the 2014 NWSL College Draft and joins the Chicago Red Stars after having scored 31 goals in 79 appearances in three years for the Broncos.

FACT FILE

DOB: 06.04.92

HEIGHT: 1.70m (5'7")

WEIGHT: 61kg (134lb)

USA: Caps **95** Goals **19**

POSITION: **Midfielder**

CLUBS: Chicago Red Stars (current), Santa Clara Broncos

2015
She is a late call-up to the USA squad for the World Cup and is one of five players to play every minute as they lift the trophy.

2017
A memorable year for Ertz as she wins the United States Women's National Soccer Team (USWNT) Player of the Year award.

2019
Ertz plays a pivotal role as USA win a second successive World Cup.

DID YOU KNOW?
Ertz runs the Ertz Family Foundation, a charity that provides grants to Philadelphia non-profit organisations and which offers help to Haitian orphans.

FERNANDINHO

Fernando Luiz Roza, known as Fernandinho, is an incredibly important player for Manchester City. On the pitch, he covers every blade of grass to help break down opposing attacks before releasing the ball to City's creative players. His effectiveness was perfectly measured when, in his absence midway through the 2018/19 season due to a thigh injury, City suffered consecutive defeats against Crystal Palace and Leicester City. On his return, City lost just one domestic match until the end of the season. More recently, he showed his reading of the game and versatility by slotting seamlessly into City's defence in the absence of the injured John Stones and Aymeric Laporte.

'If a team has three Fernandinhos, they would be champions. We have one, but he is fast, he is intelligent, he is strong in the air, he can play several positions.'

Manchester City boss Pep Guardiola

HIGHLIGHTS

2005
Fernandinho joins Ukranian club Shakhtar Donetsk from Athletico Paranaense, with whom he was a runner-up in the Brazilian first division (2004) and Libertadores de América (2005).

2006
At the end of his first season, in which he played 34 matches in all competitions, Fernandinho scores a goal for Shakhtar against Dynamo Kyiv that helps them win the title, Fernandinho's first with the club.

2008
In his third season, Fernandinho scores 11 goals as Shakhtar reclaim the title from rivals Kyiv and win the Ukrainian Cup.

2009
A year later, Fernandinho scores another 11 goals, including a crucial strike in the UEFA Cup semi-final, before Shakhtar go on to lift the cup with victory over German club Werder Bremen in the final.

FACT FILE

DOB: 04.05.85

HEIGHT: 1.75m (5'9")

WEIGHT: 66kg (146lb)

BRAZIL: Caps 53 Goals 2

POSITION: Defensive midfielder

CLUBS: Manchester City (current), Athletico Paranaense, Shakhtar Donetsk

2012
The silverware continues. He ends the campaign with a third consecutive league title and two cup winners' medals.

2013
The Brazilian joins Manchester City and he wins his first trophy in March 2014, the league cup, with a win against Sunderland. Two months later, City win the league title.

2018
Fernandinho wins his second league title at City, his three goals and three assists contributing to the club's third ever league victory.

FAMOUS FOR...
In the dressing room, Fernandinho has been, and continues to be, a positive influence on his Brazilian teammates.

33

ROBERTO
FIRMINO

Football is full of rags-to-riches stories and Brazilian ace Roberto Firmino is a classic example. As a child, he often trained on an empty stomach when food was scarce at home, and he sold coconuts on the beach for cash. Now, though, he's the highest scoring Brazilian in the history of the Premier League, a Champions League winner with Liverpool, and one of the best strikers in the world. Firmino

'He's an incredibly important player. He enjoys it so much to play in this team, to be really there with all these super guys around him. He's a very valuable player for us.'

Jürgen Klopp on Roberto 'Bobby' Firmino

combines a natural level of skill and creativity honed on the beaches of home with a hard-work ethic developed during a spell with German club Hoffenheim. The result is a No. 9 his manager Jürgen Klopp describes as the 'engine' of his Liverpool side.

HIGHLIGHTS

2008
After scoring two overhead kicks in his trial, Firmino joins his first club Figueirense aged 17. He makes his professional debut a year later.

2010
Scores his first professional goal in a win away at São Caetano. He joins Hoffenheim in December that year.

2014
He makes his international debut in a 4–0 win against Turkey. He scores his first international goal four days later, against Austria.

2015
Joins Liverpool. In his last 66 games at Hoffenheim, Firmino played a part – either by scoring or creating – in 45 goals.

FACT FILE

DOB: 02.10.91

HEIGHT: 1.80m (5'11")

WEIGHT: 76kg (168lb)

BRAZIL: Caps **44** Goals **13**

POSITION: Forward

CLUBS: Liverpool (current), Figueirense, 1899 Hoffenheim

2018
Firmino ends the 2017/18 campaign with 27 goals in all competitions, his most prolific season to date.

2019
Shortly after scoring his first hat-trick for Liverpool, in December 2018, Firmino scores Liverpool's 1,000th goal at Anfield in the Premier League era.

2019
In August, after winning the Copa América with Brazil in the summer, Firmino becomes the first Brazilian player to register 50 goals in the Premier League.

FAMOUS FOR...
Firmino has perfected the art of the 'no-look' goal, where he scores while looking in a different direction.

PERNILLE
HARDER

It was business as usual for VfL Wolfsburg and striker Pernille Harder halfway through the 2019/20 Frauen-Bundesliga season. Wolfsburg topped the league and looked on course for a fourth consecutive league title, while Harder – the 2018 UEFA Women's Player of the Year – had scored four more goals than her nearest competitor to reach 18, the same figure that saw her finish second in the goalscoring charts for the whole of 2018/19. Finishing first is something Harder has become used to; she has won three league titles and three cups with Wolfsburg, league and cup winners' medals in Sweden with Linköpings, and she starred as Denmark reached the 2017 European Championship final … an achievement that has sparked a growth in women's football in the country.

'I always dreamed of being one of the biggest players in women's football and of being able to change things.'

Pernille Harder

HIGHLIGHTS

2010
Harder signs for Danish side Skovbakken in April. Two years later, she moves to Swedish club Linköpings. The highlight of her first 12 months is scoring four goals in one game, against Sunnanå.

2011
Harder continues her fine goalscoring record for Denmark by netting two hat-tricks against Austria and Armenia.

2013
Another hat-trick on international duty takes Harder's tally in Denmark's Euro 2013 qualifying campaign to nine, more than that of any other player.

2015
Harder scores 17 goals in 22 appearances for Linköpings, a campaign that earns her a number of personal accolades, including Forward of the Year. She also wins the Danish Footballer of the Year award.

FACT FILE

DOB: 15.11.92

HEIGHT: 1.68m (5'6")

WEIGHT: 60kg (132lb)

DENMARK: Caps 115
Goals 59

POSITION: Forward

CLUBS: VfL Wolfsburg
(current), Team Viborg, IK
Skovbakken, Linköpings

2016

A further 23 goals sees Harder win the top goalscorer and Player of the Year awards again while Linköpings lift the Damallsvenskan title. In November, she announces that she's signing for VfL Wolfsburg.

2017

Captains Denmark to the Euro 2017 final, where she scores. Hosts Netherlands win the match 4–2. She's voted runner-up in the UEFA Women's Player of the Year award.

2019

Scores back-to-back hat-tricks for Denmark and Wolfsburg in a year that sees her win a third league title with the German club.

DID YOU KNOW?

In 2009, aged just 16, Harder scored a hat-trick on her international debut, against Georgia.

EDEN
HAZARD

In 2010, rumour has it that Real Madrid legend Zinedine Zidane asked Real president Florentino Pérez to sign Lille's then 19-year-old starlet Eden Hazard, such was the youngster's prodigious talent. It didn't happen. However, fast-forward nine years and Madrid, with Zidane as manager, finally got their man. The Belgian star has had something of a slow start to life at the Bernabéu since joining from Chelsea, but he can look back on seven years of brilliance and consistency at Stamford Bridge, where he scored 110 goals in 352 appearances and won the Player of the Year award for a second time in his final season. He left after scoring two goals in his last game, a 4–1 win against Arsenal in the Europa League final, two of 21 goals in 2018/19, his best return in a Chelsea shirt.

> *'After Messi and Ronaldo, Hazard is my favourite player. It is spectacular to see him play.'*
>
> Real Madrid boss Zinedine Zidane

HIGHLIGHTS

2005
Hazard starts his senior career at Ligue 1 Lille, making his professional debut in 2007. At the end of his first full season, he wins the Ligue 1 Young Player of the Year, becoming the first non-French player to do so.

2008
Hazard makes his senior international debut against Luxembourg in November aged 17. He has to wait three years for his first international goal.

2011
Hazard wins a league and cup double with Lille and is named the Ligue 1 Player of the Year, the youngest player to receive the award.

2012
The Belgian joins Chelsea and wins the Europa League in his first season. Twelve months later, he wins the Professional Footballer's Association (PFA) Young Player of the Year award.

FACT FILE

DOB: 07.01.91

HEIGHT: 1.75m (5'9")

WEIGHT: 70kg (154lb)

BELGIUM: Caps **106** Goals **32**

POSITION: Attacking midfielder

CLUBS: Real Madrid (current), Lille, Chelsea

2015

Chelsea win a league and league cup double and Hazard is key to the Blues' success. He wins the Football Writers' Association (FWA) Footballer of the Year and PFA Players' Player of the Year awards.

2017

Hazard wins his second league title with Chelsea.

2018

After winning the FA Cup with Chelsea, Hazard captains Belgium to third place at the 2018 World Cup in Russia, their best finish in history. A year later, after winning the Europa League, he joins Real Madrid.

DID YOU KNOW?

Eden Hazard's first competitive game, which he played at the age of 10 against a girls' team, ended up in a disappointing 5–0 loss.

TOBIN
HEATH

Tobin Heath was one of four members of USA's victorious women's World Cup squad – alongside Megan Rapinoe, Alex Morgan and Rose Lavelle – named among the nominees for the Ballon d'Or Feminin in 2019. Heath contributed one assist for USA in France and her club stats were equally as modest, scoring three goals and contributing three assists in 13 matches for Portland Thorns. Compare this to her seven goals and six assists in 10 games for USA in 2018 and you'd think she'd had a poor year. However, Heath has an ability to get fans out of their seats with her dribbling ability, speed, passion and willingness to take risks. Of those three club goals in 2019, for example, one was an audacious backheel, against Sky Blue FC. That's Heath all over: box office gold.

> *'One of my favorite things about soccer is how the art and the passion of the game somehow unites people and nations and classes and races.'*
>
> Tobin Heath

HIGHLIGHTS

2005
Heath joins New Jersey Wildcats and helps them win the USL W-League Championship in 2005.

2006
While at the University of North Carolina, Heath helps the university team win the NCAA Division I Women's Soccer Championship title. She wins it again in 2008 and 2009.

2008
Heath is one of three college athletes to represent USA's gold medal-winning team at the Beijing Olympics. She plays three games. It's the first of two Olympic golds.

2010
Heath is the first pick of the 2010 College Draft and she's selected by Atlanta Beat. Later that year, she joins Sky Blue FC.

FACT FILE

DOB: 29.05.88

HEIGHT: 1.68m (5'6")

WEIGHT: 59kg (130lb)

USA: Caps **162** Goals **32**

POSITION: Forward

CLUBS: Portland Thorns (current), New Jersey Wildcats, Hudson Valley Quickstrike Lady Blues, Pali Blues, Atlanta Beat, Sky Blue FC, New York Fury, Paris Saint-Germain

2013
Joins Paris Saint-Germain on a six-month deal. She returns for a second spell from Portland Thorns later in the year. Heath scores the winning goal for the Thorns that secures the NWSL Championship.

2015
Starts five of USA's seven games and scores in the World Cup final as the team beats Japan, the team that defeated them in the 2011 final, to lift the first of two consecutive World Cup titles.

2018
After missing the start of the 2018 campaign, Heath scores seven goals and adds seven assists in the regular season, and scores in the play-off semi-final. She's named in the NWSL Best XI.

FAMOUS FOR...
Nutmegs! No one loves putting the ball through an opponent's legs – or a teammate's in training – than Heath, so much so that it has become her signature move.

ADA
HEGERBERG

Ada Hegerberg has scored so many goals and won so many trophies that you'd be forgiven for thinking she was older than 24. Since moving to France in 2014, the prolific forward has won five league titles,

'She has unconventional qualities. It is impressive how she has managed to make history in such a short space of time.'
Lyon teammate Eugénie Le Sommer

six cups and four European titles. In 2018, she was the first-ever recipient of the Ballon d'Or Féminin, and she accepted the award with a speech in two languages that aren't her mother tongue. In 2019, she was named BBC Women's Footballer of the Year before overtaking Anja Mittag as the highest scorer in the Women's Champions League with 53 goals from 50 games, and the fastest player – male or female – to reach 50 goals in European action. For context, Lionel Messi did it in 66 games, Cristiano Ronaldo in 91.

HIGHLIGHTS

2011
Aged 15, Hegerberg helps Norway reach the 2011 U19 European Championship final. She turns 16 in July, and becomes the youngest player to score a hat-trick in Norway's top division.

2012
Hegerberg top scores in the league once more, this time as a Stabaek player, with 25 goals in 18 matches.

2014
Hegerberg joins Olympique Lyonnais and scores 26 goals in 22 games in her first season as Lyon claim a ninth consecutive league title and win a league and cup double.

2015
Hegerberg finishes the season atop the goal charts again, this time with 33 in 21 appearances. She wins a league, cup and Champions League treble, scoring 13 times in nine European games.

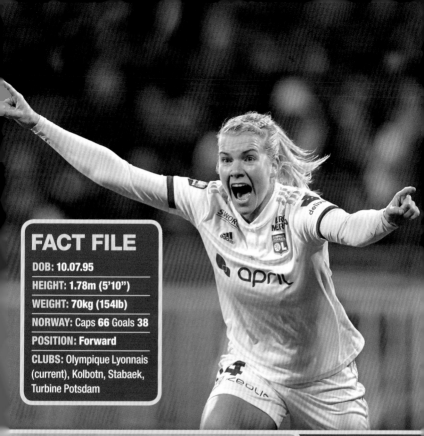

FACT FILE

DOB: 10.07.95

HEIGHT: 1.78m (5'10")

WEIGHT: 70kg (154lb)

NORWAY: Caps **66** Goals **38**

POSITION: Forward

CLUBS: Olympique Lyonnais (current), Kolbotn, Stabaek, Turbine Potsdam

2016
Hegerberg is awarded the Norwegian Golden Ball for 2015 for being the best footballer – male or female – in Norway, the first time for a female in 20 years.

2017
Despite having scored 38 goals in 66 internationals, Hederberg stops representing Norway as a form of protest against the Norwegian Football Federation (NFF) for the way they treat women's football.

2018
Becomes the first ever winner of the Ballon d'Or Féminin. A year later, the Norwegian becomes the first player to score three goals in a women's Champions League final as Lyon beats Barcelona to won a fourth consecutive European title.

DID YOU KNOW?
Hegerberg remains eighth in Norway's list of all-time top scorers despite not having played for her country since 2017.

AMANDINE HENRY

One of the best players in the world playing at the best club in the world, Amandine Henry is a powerful force, the complete defensive midfielder. She can tackle and break up play, but she can also orchestrate and dictate attacks with her incisive passing and intensity. She's a natural leader who knows what it takes to win, captaining both club and country and enjoying plenty of silverware at a domestic level. At Lyon, for example, she has won 11 league titles, seven French cups and five Champions League trophies. In between her two spells at Lyon, she won a National Women's Soccer League (NWSL) title and a NWSL shield with Portland Thorns.

> 'She's fantastic, I consider her one of the best players in the world. She has this competitiveness. She is a natural leader.'
>
> Former Portland Thorns teammate Tobin Heath

HIGHLIGHTS

2004
Amandine started playing football aged five and after a decade of playing against boys, in the absence of a girls' team, she joined her first club, Hénin-Beaumont. A year later, Henry joins the French football academy.

2007
Aged 18, Henry joins Lyon, the most successful club in France. She gets injured with a knee problem in her first season and considers giving up the game.

2008
A year later, however, she wins her first Division 1 Féminine title, the first of eight consecutive league wins that follow. A year later, she makes her international debut for France.

2013
After being dropped from the France team, Henry returns. Four years later she's given the captain's armband.

44

FACT FILE

DOB: 28.09.89

HEIGHT: 1.70m (5'7")

WEIGHT: 64kg (141lb)

FRANCE: Caps **88** Goals **13**

POSITION: Midfield

CLUBS: Olympique Lyonnais (current), Hénin-Beaumont, CNFE Clairefontaine, Olympique Lyonnais, Portland Thorns, Paris Saint-Germain

2015
Awarded the Silver Ball Award for being the second best player of the Women's World Cup in Canada. She is also voted into the World Cup all-star team, and later into the FIFA FIFPro World XI.

2016
The midfielder joins Portland Thorns. A year later, she becomes an NWSL champion as her side beats North Carolina Courage to win the 2017 championship.

2019
Henry leads France into a World Cup on home soil and scores two crucial goals; in the first game against South Korea, and a dramatic winner in the last 16 against Brazil.

DID YOU KNOW?
Henry is a danger at both ends of the pitch, and when she scores it's often spectacular. In fact, scoring from long range has become something of a trademark.

JENNIFER HERMOSO

The Spanish forward enjoyed an incredible spell in front of goal in 2019. She scored 27 league goals for Atlético Madrid and Barcelona either side of a World Cup in which she scored three times for Spain, taking her tally for the year to 41 in all competitions. Finding the net is something Jenni finds easy. Her best return came in a four-year spell at Barcelona in which she scored 77 goals in 90 games. A relatively quiet year at Paris Saint-Germain followed before she netted 18 in 21 games during her second stint at hometown club Atlético. And now, midway through the Spanish domestic season, she's already struck 15 goals in 13 games. Only Pernille Harder at Wolfsburg had scored more at the same stage in Europe.

'What we have fought for is for women to play in big stadiums with many people watching … and to be the mirror of those girls that want to start playing football.'

Jennifer Hermoso talking to FIFA

HIGHLIGHTS

2006
Hermoso spends four years at Atlético Madrid after joining in 2006, from where she joins Rayo Vallecano. After a spell in Sweden in 2013, she returns to Spain.

2011
The Spaniard earns her first call-up to the national team. Two years later, she plays and scores at the Women's Euros in Sweden as Spain are knocked out by Norway in the quarter-finals.

2013
Hermoso joins Barcelona, where she wins two Primera Division titles and two Copa de la Reina cup winners' medals in four years. She scores her first international goal for Spain, against Russia.

2014
Scores her first international hat-trick in a 10–0 win against North Macedonia in World Cup qualification.

FACT FILE

DOB: 09.05.80

HEIGHT: 1.75m (5'9")

WEIGHT: 59kg (130lb)

SPAIN: Caps **68** Goals **30**

POSITION: Forward

CLUBS: FC Barcelona (current), Atlético Madrid, Rayo Vallecano, Tyresö FF, FC Barcelona, Paris Saint-Germain, Atlético Madrid

2017
The attacking midfielder joins Paris Saint-Germain on a three-year deal but leaves after one season, in which PSG finish second in the league but win the Coupe de France.

2018
Hermoso returns to her first club Atlético before rejoining Barcelona for a second time.

2019
Scores twice in Spain's opening fixture of the 2019 World Cup in France, against South Africa. She also scores in the last 16 defeat against USA.

DID YOU KNOW?
Hermoso has averaged a goal every 63 minutes for Spain.

SON
HEUNG-MIN

The Tottenham Hotspur striker seems to get better every season. South Korean international Son is lightning quick, two-footed and he scores vital – and often

'He works so hard, always pushing, never gives up. He will try try try try try.'

Former Tottenham boss Mauricio Pochettino

spectacular – goals in big games. He has scored 15 or more times in three of his last four campaigns and looked set to continue that record in 2019/20, scoring or creating 13 goals, until he was injured in January 2020. Son, Asia's solitary Ballon d'Or nominee in 2019, evoked memories of Diego Maradona's famous run on goal against England in 1986 when, against Burnley, Son dribbled the ball on a scintillating 70m (77 yard) dash before finishing clinically. Son's goals were crucial in helping Spurs reach the Champions League final in 2018/19. He netted a vital goal against Borussia Dortmund in the last 16 in particular, before netting a further three in the two-legged quarter-final victory against Manchester City.

HIGHLIGHTS

2010
After joining Hamburg's academy in 2009 he scores nine goals in pre-season and signs his first professional contract on his 18th birthday. He becomes Hamburg's youngest ever goalscorer in October 2010.

2012
Son starts the 2011/12 season with 18 goals in nine pre-season matches and scores five in 30 league matches, including two crucial goals against Hannover 96 and FC Nürnberg that help keep Hamburg in the Bundesliga.

2013
Son becomes the fifth Korean footballer to score 10 or more goals in a season in Europe, before signing for Bayer 04 Leverkusen for a club record fee of €10m.

2015
After scoring a goal every three matches, he joins Tottenham Hotspur and, at £22m, he becomes the most expensive Asian footballer in history.

FACT FILE

DOB: 08.07.92

HEIGHT: 1.83m (6'0")

WEIGHT: 77kg (170lb)

SOUTH KOREA:
Caps **87** Goals **26**

POSITION: Forward

CLUBS: Tottenham Hotspur
(current), Hamburger SV
II, Hamburger SV, Bayer 04
Leverkusen

2016
After a disappointing
first season he
comes to life in
the second, and in
September becomes
the first Korean to
win a Premier League
Player of the Month
award. He wins
another in April.

2018
Son captains South
Korea to victory in
the Asian Games.
Their win in the
final, against Japan,
exempts the whole
squad from doing
military service.

2019
Son becomes the
highest scoring
Asian player in the
Champions League
after he registers
his 12th goal in the
competition, against
Manchester City.
He's later shortlisted
for the Ballon d'Or.

DID YOU KNOW?
Son was the first
player to score at
Tottenham's new
stadium when he
netted the opener
against Crystal
Palace in April 2019.

HARRY KANE

Harry Kane is one of the most feared strikers in football, but he has had to work hard to reach the top. At the start of his career, he spent time on loan to four different clubs in an attempt to gain more experience. By November 2019, he was Tottenham's third highest goalscorer of all time. In 2017/18, Kane scored 41 goals in total and became the first Spurs player to hit 30-plus goals in a Premier League campaign. In 2018/19, he became the first Spurs player to hit 100 goals in the Premier League, and then overtook Alessandro Del Piero to become the fastest player to hit 20 goals in the Champions League. For England, which he captains, he top scored at the World Cup in Russia in 2018. Then, in qualifying for Euro 2020, he became the first Three Lions player to score in every match in a qualifying campaign.

'For a youngster to be able to study him and see his professionalism and the way he works at his game, he's an incredible example.'
England manager Gareth Southgate

HIGHLIGHTS

2004
Kane joins Tottenham's academy at the second time of applying following an unsuccessful trial, and this after unsuccessful trials with both Watford and Arsenal.

2009
Kane signs scholar forms for Spurs on his 16th birthday, and signs professional forms a year later.

2011
In January, Kane joins Leyton Orient on loan, the first of four spells away from Tottenham. He scores five goals in 18 games.

2012
After scoring seven goals in 22 games at Millwall, Kane joins Norwich City, then Leicester City in 2013.

FACT FILE

DOB: 28.07.93

HEIGHT: 1.88m (6'2")

WEIGHT: 86kg (190lb)

ENGLAND: Caps 45 Goals 32

POSITION: Forward

CLUBS: Tottenham Hotspur (current), Leyton Orient (loan), Millwall (loan), Norwich City (loan), Leicester City (loan)

2013
Scores his first goal for Spurs, in a League Cup tie against Hull. He's given his first Premier League start a year later, against Sunderland, and scores.

2015
Kane is voted the PFA Players' Player of the Year. A year later, he wins the Golden Boot as the Premier League's top scorer, with 25 goals.

2017
Kane wins a second consecutive Golden Boot and becomes only the fifth player to do so. Two years later, Kane becomes England's highest-ever scoring captain.

DID YOU KNOW?
Kane was appointed a Member of the Order of the British Empire (MBE) in 2019 for services to football.

51

N'GOLO
KANTÉ

If there were one footballer you would entrust with the task of winning the ball back with your team out of possession, it would be N'Golo Kanté. What's more, the Frenchman simply never stops running. His international teammate Paul Pogba once joked that Kanté has '15 lungs', while Kanté himself once told his Leicester City teammates that he was considering running to training. Yet there's more to his game than his world-class defensive midfield duties. Kanté, who won consecutive Premier League titles in 2016 and 2017 at two different clubs, Leicester City and Chelsea, before winning the World Cup with France in 2018, can also play in a more advanced position, out wide and even contributes with important goals in key games.

> *'He never stopped running in training. I tell him: 'One day, I'm going to see you cross the ball, and then finish the cross with a header yourself'.'*
>
> Former Leicester City manager Claudio Ranieri

HIGHLIGHTS

2012
Kanté makes his professional debut as a substitute for Boulogne. After the side are relegated, he spends one season in Division 3 before joining Caen on a free transfer in Division 2.

2014
Caen finish third and win promotion to Ligue 1. Kanté spends one season in the French top flight and wins the ball back more than any other player in Europe, before joining Leicester City for just £5.6m.

2015
He wins the Premier League in his first season in England and wins the Player of the Year award.

2016
Kanté makes his international debut for France and is part of the squad that finish runners-up at the 2016 European Championship.

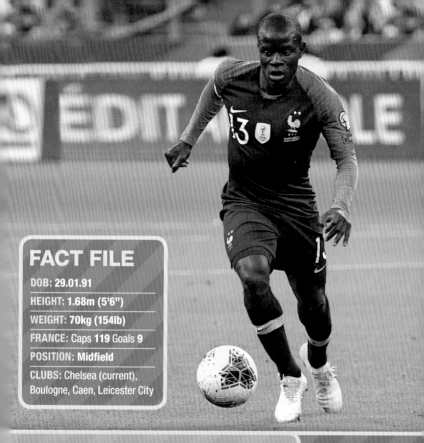

FACT FILE

DOB: 29.01.91

HEIGHT: 1.68m (5'6")

WEIGHT: 70kg (154lb)

FRANCE: Caps **119** Goals **9**

POSITION: Midfield

CLUBS: Chelsea (current), Boulogne, Caen, Leicester City

2017

Moves to Chelsea for £32m. He wins the league for a second time, and in doing so becomes the first outfield player since Eric Cantona to win consecutive titles with different clubs. He wins the PFA Players' Player and FWA Footballer of the Year awards.

2018

Kanté wins the FA Cup after victory against Manchester United, and he's later nominated for the Ballon d'Or award.

2018

Kanté is an important player for France as they win the 2018 World Cup in Russia. He plays all seven matches, including the final against Croatia.

FAMOUS FOR…

Kanté had famously spent most of his career playing in the French second and third divisions, spending one year in Ligue 1 before joining Leicester City.

SAMANTHA KERR

Australia 2005 and somebody, somewhere is responsible for a 12-year-old Sam Kerr receiving a black eye while playing Aussie Rules football, Australia's most famous contact sport. This is significant, for it proves a turning point, when Kerr's parents steer her towards football as we know it instead. It was a good decision, for Kerr is now one of the most prolific strikers in the world. She's the current all-time leading scorer in both the USA's National Women's Soccer League (NWSL) with 69 goals and Australia's W-League (70 goals), and she is a four-time winner of the Professional Footballers' Association (PFA) Women's Footballer of the Year award.

'Sam has proved time and time again in the NWSL that she is a prolific goalscorer. She's won the Golden Boot many times and she's a player that can make things happen, but she's also a fantastic team player.'

Chelsea manager Emma Hayes

HIGHLIGHTS

2008
Kerr joins Perth Glory from Western Knights and makes her full debut aged 15. A year later, Kerr is voted Players' Player of the Year and wins the goal of the year award. She also makes her international debut against Italy.

2013
Kerr joins Western New York Flash and scores six goals in 19 starts. She wins the W-League with Sydney FC later that year.

2014
Kerr wins the W-League again, this time with Perth Glory.

2017
Kerr scores four goals in one game and finishes the season with 17 goals to top the NWSL scoring charts.

54

FACT FILE

DOB: 10.09.93

HEIGHT: 1.68m (5'6")

WEIGHT: 55kg (121lb)

AUSTRALIA: Caps **83** Goals **38**

POSITION: Forward

CLUBS: Chelsea (current), Perth Glory, Sydney FC, Western New York Flash, Sky Blue, Chicago Red Stars

2018
Kerr joins Chicago Red Stars, scores 16 goals and wins her second consecutive Golden Boot.

2019
Kerr nets 17 goals for Perth Glory, then 18 goals – and a third consecutive Golden Boot – for the Red Stars. She wins the NWSL Most Valuable Player (MVP), the first player to do so twice.

2019
Kerr scores four goals in one game, against Jamaica, and five in total at the 2019 World Cup in France.

FAMOUS FOR…
Chelsea fans will love it when Kerr finds the net, for the Aussie likes to celebrate with an iconic backflip goal celebration.

FRANCESCA KIRBY

Described as 'Mini Messi' at the 2015 World Cup in Canada by then England coach Mark Sampson, and more recently talked up by current boss Phil Neville ahead of the 2019 World Cup in France, forward Fran Kirby has star quality but is often hindered by injuries. However, when fit and firing, there's no question that the diminutive forward – who can also play wide – is one of the most exciting attacking players in England. When Kirby joined Chelsea from Reading in 2015, she signed for between £40–60k, which was a then WSL record. Kirby can create moments of magic out of nothing and score spectacular goals. In 2018, she won a league and FA Cup double and won two individual awards alongside being nominated for the Ballon d'Or Feminin. Injuries and a heart condition stifled Kirby once again in 2019, but 2020 promises to be better.

> **'She's a wonderful talent.'**
> Chelsea manager Emma Hayes

HIGHLIGHTS

2000
Kirby joins hometown club Reading aged just seven and works her way up through the youth teams.

2012
After taking a break from the game, Kirby returns and finishes the 2012/13 season with 32 goals in 21 appearances and the FA Women's Premier League Southern Division as top scorer.

2014
Kirby helps Reading finish third in the newly formed Women's Super League 2 with 24 goals in 16 appearances, and again finishes top of the division's scoring charts. She's later named the WSL2 Players' Player of the Year.

2015
After scoring on her England debut in 2014, Kirby is called up to the England squad for the 2015 World Cup in Canada. She scores in a 2–1 win against Mexico. England finish third.

FACT FILE

DOB: 29.06.93

HEIGHT: 1.57m (5'2")

WEIGHT: 52kg (115lb)

ENGLAND: Caps **45**
Goals **13**

POSITION: Forward

CLUBS: Chelsea
(current), Reading

2015
Kirby scored 11 goals in five games before joining Chelsea, where she scored twice in a 4–0 win against Sunderland to help Chelsea secure the FA WSL. She also scored Chelsea's first goal in the Women's Champions League.

2018
Kirby is awarded the PFA players' Player of the Year award and the Football Writers' Women's Footballer of the Year awards.

2019
Kirby plays in her third major tournament for England, the 2019 World Cup in France, following the World Cup in 2015 and European Championship in 2017.

DID YOU KNOW?
Kirby has been battling mental health challenges ever since her mum died when she was 14. Opening up about her vulnerability has seemingly helped Kirby.

SAKI
KUMAGAI

Japanese defender/midfielder Saki Kumagai might need a bigger trophy cabinet. In 2019, she won three trophies with Olympique Lyonnais before adding the AFC Women's Player of the Year award to an already impressive collection that includes a World Cup winners' medal, an Asian Cup winners' medal and an Olympic silver.

'Football for me is joy. If football didn't exist I couldn't express myself – it's my life. Without football life is less interesting and too serious. You always have to laugh.'

Saki Kumagai

The classy midfielder played 20 games for a start-studded Lyon side as they won a record 17th Division 1 Féminine title in 2019, her sixth since she joined the club in 2013, a record sixth Champions League (Kumagai's fourth) and a record 10th Coupe de France Féminine (her fifth). Kumagai will lead the next generation of Japanese players at the Tokyo Olympics.

HIGHLIGHTS

2008
Kumagai makes her debut for the Japan national team, against Canada, aged just 17. Later that year, she plays for Japan's U20s at the U20 World Cup.

2009
Joins Japanese club Urawa Red Diamonds and the club wins the Japanese Nadeshiko Championship in her first season. She plays 21 league games.

2011
Two years later, Kumagai moves to German Bundesliga club Frankfurt, where she spends two seasons and plays 75 games. Japan wins the World Cup and Kumagai scores the winning penalty to defeat USA.

2012
Plays in her first of two Olympic Games (it will be three if she plays in Tokyo). Japan finish with a silver medal after losing to USA in the final.

FACT FILE

DOB: 17.10.90

HEIGHT: 1.73m (5'8")

WEIGHT: 60kg (132lb)

JAPAN: Caps **110** Goals **1**

POSITION: Defender/midfielder

CLUBS: Olympique Lyonnais (current), Frankfurt, Urawa Red Diamonds

2013
Moves to French club Olympique Lyonnais and wins a Ligue 1 winners' medal in her first season. Lyon also lift the Coupe de France.

2016
Lyon dominate both home and abroad by winning a Ligue 1, Coupe de France and Women's Champions League treble.

2017
Kumagai enjoys her best season in front of goal, netting 11 times in all competitions as Lyon once again win a treble. She's also named Japan captain.

DID YOU KNOW?
Aged 20, Kumagai scored the decisive spot kick that saw Japan beat USA in the World Cup final penalty shootout in 2011. Five years later, she scored the winning penalty in a Champions League final.

ROSE
LAVELLE

It speaks volumes for Rose Lavelle's ability that in 2019 the Cincinnati-born attacking midfielder managed to stand out in a squad full of superstars as USA won a second consecutive World Cup. She scored a memorable goal in the final against the Netherlands and netted three times from seven shots in the competition overall.

'Every time she crosses that white line, she's going out there to have fun. But at the same time, she's quick, she has great vision, she can pass the ball, she can shoot.'

Former coach Matt Beard

Yet it was her trickery and wizardry, combined with a willingness to run at players, that won over the hearts of a nation, and that puts her in at the forefront to lead USA going into the Tokyo Olympics in 2020 and beyond. Lavelle is small in size but big in stature, and she's so comfortable with the ball at her feet that defenders cannot take their eyes off her for a second.

HIGHLIGHTS

2013
Lavelle attends the University of Wisconsin–Madison and, following her exploits with the football team, is named Freshman of the Year and first-team All-American by the National Soccer Coaches Association of America (NSCAA).

2014
Lavelle dominates at the U20 CONCACAF Championships where USA score 29 goals and concede none in five games. She wins the Golden Ball as the tournament's best player.

2015
Lavelle plays Summer League football while at university, first for the Dayton Dutch Lions and then Seattle Sounders Women.

2017
Lavelle is drafted by the Boston Breakers and she scores two goals in her first eight games before picking up an injury that limits the amount of games she plays.

FACT FILE

DOB: 14.05.95

HEIGHT: 1.63m (5'4")

WEIGHT: 55kg (121lb)

USA: Caps **38** Goals **10**

POSITION: Attacking midfielder

CLUBS: Washington Spirit (current), Dayton Dutch Lions, Seattle Sounders, Boston Breakers

2017
She also makes her senior international debut, against England, at the SheBelieves Cup, and is named Player of the Match.

2018
Lavelle joins Washington Spirit, for whom she has played 17 games and scored one goal in two seasons. She also scores three goals in five games for USA at the 2018 CONCACAF Women's Championship.

2019
Lavelle starts six games for USA at the 2019 World Cup and scores three goals. Her dazzling performances see her awarded the Bronze Ball as the tournament's third best player.

DID YOU KNOW?
Lavelle has a bulldog named Wilma, and she loves to share its weight-loss travails and fashion 'choices' across her social media channels.

EUGÉNIE
LE SOMMER

With football in her blood, it's no surprise that French star Eugénie Le Sommer has become a goal machine and a poster girl for women's football in France. Both her parents played football, her mum Claudine representing French giants Paris Saint-Germain in the 1980s. And while her mum continued to play amateur football until she was 47, Eugénie has benefited from the professionalism of women's football in France since 2010. She joined Olympique Lyonnais that summer and has since won nine league titles, seven cups and six Champions League titles, 24 titles in total. At the time of writing, Le Sommer was closing in on Marinette Pichon's record of 81 goals as the highest ever goalscorer for 'Les Bleus'.

'I'm fast and technical. I'm small. Yes, I'm a small player so — I am not physically that strong as the others, so I have to adapt... With my feet, I'm very quick.'

Eugénie Le Sommer

HIGHLIGHTS

2007
Le Sommer joins Stade Briochin after playing for several clubs at a youth level. She scores four goals in 22 games in her debut season.

2009
After scoring 10 goals in 22 matches in 2008/09, she starts the next season with 10 goals in the first seven games. She finishes the campaign as the league's top scorer.

2011
Le Sommer ends her first season at Olympique Lyonnais with 17 goals. She scores 22 goals the following season, and 20 the year after that.

2015
Le Sommer enjoys her most profitable season in front of goal, scoring 29 times in the French league.

FACT FILE

DOB: 18.05.89

HEIGHT: 1.60m (5'3")

WEIGHT: 58kg (128lb)

FRANCE: Caps **167** Goals **80**

POSITION: Midfield/forward

CLUBS: Olympique Lyonnais (current), Lorient, Stade Briochin

2018
Le Sommer overtakes Lotta Schelin to become Lyon's top scorer of all time thanks to a hat-trick scored against Toulouse.

2019
After scoring two goals for France at the World Cup on home soil, Le Sommer shows little sign of slowing down in front of goal, scoring seven goals in her first five games of the 2019/20 season.

2020
Ahead of the Tournoi de France in March, and France facing Brazil, a documentary about Le Sommer and her life and career was broadcast across the country.

DID YOU KNOW?
Le Sommer is one of seven children. She has four sisters and two brothers.

ROBERT LEWANDOWSKI

A player who admits he's 'addicted to scoring goals', Robert Lewandowski has been an unstoppable force in 2019/20; his most fruitful campaign in an already incredibly prolific career. After signing a new contract at Bayern Munich, ending speculation he might leave, Lewandowski started as he meant to go on with seven goals in five games in August. By early November, he had scored in every Bundesliga and Champions League game he'd played in, bagged the quickest quadruple – in 14 minutes and 31 seconds – in Champions League history and become Bayern's all-time record scorer in European action, and even netted more goals than five Bundesliga clubs! That's a goal every 109 minutes. And all of this despite Bayern failing to reach top gear.

> *'My passport might say that I'm 31, but I don't feel my age. I'm only just coming into my prime and hopefully, it'll last a few more years. The best is still to come.'*
>
> Robert Lewandowski

HIGHLIGHTS

2010
Lewandowski ends the 2009/10 season with a league winners' medal and atop the goalscoring charts in Poland's top division with 18 goals.

2013
Wins his second successive league winners' medal following his move to Borussia Dortmund in 2010. He finishes the 2012/13 season with 22 league goals and a hat-trick in the German cup final to secure Dortmund's first league and cup double.

2014
He finishes the 2013/14 campaign as the top scorer in the Bundesliga with 20 goals, and 28 goals in all competitions. He joins Bayern Munich for the start of the 2014/15 season.

2015
Lewandowski scores five goals in eight minutes and 59 seconds to set a Bundesliga and European record. Four days later, he becomes the fastest foreign player to score 100 goals in the Bundesliga. It takes him just 168 games.

FACT FILE

DOB: 21.08.88

HEIGHT: 1.85m (6'1")

WEIGHT: 79kg (174lb)

POLAND: Caps **112** Goals **61**

POSITION: Striker

CLUBS: Bayern Munich (current), Znicz Pruszków, Lech Poznan, Borussia Dortmund

2016
Lewandowski achieves fourth place at the 2015 Ballon d'Or awards before becoming the first foreign player to score 30 goals in the Bundesliga. He finished the season with 42 goals in 51 matches.

2018
Lewandowski scores in 11 consecutive matches for Bayern. He's also voted Poland's Footballer of the Year for the seventh year in a row and tops the Bundesliga scoring charts for the third time, with 29 goals.

2019
After reaching the 40-goal landmark for the fourth successive season in 2018/19, and winning a second domestic double, he starts 2018/19 by scoring in 11 consecutive matches.

DID YOU KNOW?
Lewandowski's father Krystof was a Polish Judo champion. His mother and sister were both professional volleyball players. His wife is a World Cup medal winner in karate.

SADIO
MANÉ

Mo Salah has rightly been the poster boy of Liverpool's attack, but in 2019 Sadio Mané was unquestionably the most consistent part of what is Europe's most-feared attacking threesome. Alongside Salah and Roberto Firmino, Mané combines the trickery and quick feet of a winger with the movement and

'Since his first day he was an incredibly important player. If he stays healthy he will have an incredible career in front of him.'

Liverpool manager Jürgen Klopp

clinical finishing of a centre-forward. This combination makes him a dynamic – and sometimes unplayable – attacking force. In 2019, he helped Liverpool achieve Champions League glory in May, win the Club World Cup in December, and lead the chase for a long-awaited league title. Sandwiched between the 2018/19 and 2019/20 seasons, Mané helped take Senegal to the Africa Cup of Nations final, where they lost to Algeria. In January 2020, he was named the African Footballer of the Year.

HIGHLIGHTS

2011
Mané joins French club Metz from Senegalese football academy Académie Génération Foot. He makes 19 appearances in his first season, but Metz are relegated.

2012
Mané joins Austrian side Red Bull Salzburg, with Metz receiving their third biggest ever transfer fee. He scores his first hat-trick for the club in October, against Kalsdorf in the Austrian Cup.

2014
After scoring his third hat-trick for the club, in a cup game against Horn, he signs for Southampton in the Premier League.

2015
On the final day of the 2014/15 season, Mané scores a hat-trick against Aston Villa in two minutes and 56 seconds, a Premier League record.

FACT FILE

DOB: 10.04.92

HEIGHT: 1.75m (5'9")

WEIGHT: 69kg (152lb)

SENEGAL: Caps **69** Goals **19**

POSITION: Forward

CLUBS: Liverpool (current), Metz, Red Bull Salzburg, Southampton

2016
After finishing the 2015/16 season as Southampton's top scorer with 15 goals, he joins Liverpool for a transfer fee of £34m, the most ever paid for an African player at that time.

2017
Mané is awarded the Player of the Season award. A year later, he overtakes Demba Ba's record of 43 goals to become the highest-scoring Senegalese player in Premier League history.

2019
A big year, as Mané wins the Champions League and scores his 50th goal for Liverpool in his 100th game for the club.

DID YOU KNOW?
Mané is a popular figure in his home nation, where he has built a stadium and schools, and provides shoes, clothing and food for people in poverty.

LIEKE
MARTENS

Injury at the World Cup in France in 2019 curtailed Martens' development last year, but her form either side of her spell on the sidelines shows just what the Dutch forward is capable of. She scored seven goals in nine games in all competitions in March and April in 2019 before netting twice against Japan in a 2–1 win at the World Cup itself, her first goal a ridiculous backheel volley that caught the Japanese defence off guard. She missed the World Cup final, but she had impressed with her combination of tricks, twists and turns. In 2017, Martens was a UEFA Women's Championship winner and was named both UEFA Women's Player of the Year and FIFA Women's Player of the Year. In 2018, she won the Copa de la Reina and Copa Catalunya with Barcelona. A league title, and more, beckons in 2020.

> *'When I was young, I had no idea there were women players or what I could achieve and now we are role models.'*
>
> Lieke Martens

HIGHLIGHTS

2011
After top scoring at the U19 European Championship in 2010, Martens earns her first senior call-up, in a friendly against China.

2012
Martens joins German Bundesliga side FCR 2001 Duisburg, where she scores seven goals in 30 games.

2014
After a two-year spell at Kopparbergs/ Goteborg she joins Rosengård in 2016 and promptly wins a Swedish cup double.

2015
Netherlands qualify for the Women's World Cup for the first time, and Martens scores the country's first ever goal in the competition, a thumping effort against New Zealand.

FACT FILE

DOB: 16.12.92

HEIGHT: 1.70m (5'7")

WEIGHT: 66kg (146lb)

NETHERLANDS: Caps **110** Goals **44**

POSITION: Midfield

CLUBS: Barcelona (current), Heerenveen, VVV-Venlo, Standard Liège, Duisburg, Kopparbergs/ Goteborg, Rosengård

2017
Martens joins Barcelona and wins the Copa Catalunya. She scores twice, including in the final, as Netherlands win the 2017 European Championship. She wins the Golden Boot as the best player of the tournament.

2019
Martens helps Barcelona reach the Champions League final, where they're beaten by French side Olympique Lyonnais. She then scores two goals for Netherlands against Japan in the last 16 of the World Cup.

2020
Martens is part of the Barca team that beats reigning champions Real Sociedad 10-1 to lift the Spanish Super Cup.

DID YOU KNOW?
It should come as no surprise that Martens is so good at getting herself out of trouble on the pitch, her hero was Brazilian Ronaldinho. 'He had long hair like me and great dribbles. I loved him.' She told *The Guardian*.

VIVIANNE MIEDEMA

There are few things as inevitable as seeing Vivianne Miedema's name on the scoresheet. Put simply, if she's playing in a game of football there's a very big chance she's going to find the net. Just take her record in 2019, which followed an impressive 2018 – she scored 23 goals in the last three months, including three hat-tricks – she netted five times in her first five Arsenal games before ending the year with 52 goals in all competitions for club and country, and a league winners' medal for Arsenal. The highlight of this prolific spell was undoubtedly her performance against Bristol City in which she scored six and set up another four in an 11–1 win. Type her name into YouTube; she's not just a great goalscorer, but also a scorer of great goals.

'She has got qualities ordinary footballers don't have. She gives our team that something extra.'
Netherlands coach Roger Reijners

HIGHLIGHTS

2011
Miedema signs for SC Heerenveen aged just 15 and becomes the youngest ever player in the Dutch Eredivisie Vrouwen.

2014
The Dutch striker finishes the 2013/14 season with 39 goals and at the top of the scoring charts in the Dutch league. That summer, she signs for Bayern Munich. She also top scores at the U19 European Championship, as Netherlands win the tournament.

2015
Miedema ends her first season in Germany as part of a Bayern team who go the whole season unbeaten and win their first league title since 1976.

2015
She finishes Netherlands' World Cup qualifying campaign with 16 goals, including three goals in a 3–2 win against Italy that secures their place at their first ever World Cup.

FACT FILE

DOB: 15.07.96

HEIGHT: 1.75m (5'9")

WEIGHT: 65kg (143lb)

NETHERLANDS: Caps **87** Goals **69**

POSITION: Forward

CLUBS: Arsenal (current), SC Heerenveen, Bayern Munich

2017
After winning a second successive Dutch title, and lifting the European Championship with Netherlands, Miedema joins English side Arsenal.

2019
Miedema finishes the Women's Super League (WSL) with 22 goals, more than any other player, and is named PFA Player of the Year. In October, she scores four goals in one game, against Slavia Prague in the Champions League.

2019
In June, Miedema becomes Netherlands' all-time top scorer – male or female – after netting her 60th goal, in a World Cup game against Cameroon.

DID YOU KNOW?
At 23 years of age, Miedema is already the Netherlands' top scorer in history (male or female), with 69 goals.

DZSENIFER
MAROZSÁN

'She's the world's best player,' says England full-back Lucy Bronze, herself considered the world's best by some of her peers, of her Olympique Lyonnais teammate and roommate Dzsenifer Marozsán. Marozsán is arguably the world's best attacking midfielder, a powerhouse for club and country who scores goals and creates more. However, her career almost came to a premature end in 2018 when she suffered a blockage in one of her arteries. Thankfully, she only missed three months, and when she returned it was like she'd never been away. She even ended the 2018/19 campaign with a French league, Cup and Champions League treble, scoring 10 goals in 15 games. By January in the 2019/20 season, she'd already clocked eight goals and 10 assists in 18 games in all competitions.

'You rarely see anyone with as much ability as her. She's just got so much raw talent. She's so tricky and skilful.'

Teammate Lucy Bronze

HIGHLIGHTS

2007
Aged 14 years Marozsán becomes the youngest player to play in the Bundesliga when she makes her debut for FC Saarbrücken. Nine months later, she becomes the league's youngster scorer.

2008
Marozsán hits form in front of goal for Germany's U19s, winning the Golden Shoe at the U17s World Cup and top scoring at the U17 European Championship.

2009
After winning the German Second Division title in 2009, Marozsán joins FFC Frankfurt and the club finishes second in both 2011 and 2014. She wins the first of two DFB-Pokal cups in 2011.

2013
Marozsán forms part of the Germany team that defeats Norway to win the European Championship. Marozsán's performances see her named in the team of the tournament.

FACT FILE

DOB: 18.04.92

HEIGHT: 1.70m (5'7")

WEIGHT: 67kg (148lb)

GERMANY: Caps **97** Goals **32**

POSITION: Midfield

CLUBS: Olympique Lyonnais (current), FC Saarbrücken, FFC Frankfurt

2015

After winning her second DFB-Pokal Cup winners' medal, in 2014, Marozsán inspires Frankfurt to Champions League victory in 2015.

2016

Marozsán joins French club Olympique Lyonnais and in her first season the side wins a league, cup and European treble. She also wins Olympic gold with Germany.

2019

Wins the German Football of the Year award for a third time, after having already won it in 2017 and 2018. Enjoys a second treble with Lyon before heading to the World Cup with Germany.

DID YOU KNOW?

Marozsán's dad and brother both played professional football. Her dad won four caps for Hungary, while her brother was forced to retire at a young age.

ALEX MORGAN

One of the most famous faces of USA women's team and women's football generally, and a prolific striker in front of goal, Morgan is targeting her comeback from pregnancy at the Tokyo Olympics in 2020. Whether she makes it or not remains to be seen, but there's no doubting USA are more effective in front of goal with Morgan leading the line. She scored six goals at the 2019 World Cup to help USA win it for a second successive time, including five in one game against Thailand, and the decisive winner against England in the semi-final. In total, she has scored 107 goals in 169 games for her country. A born winner, Morgan won the inaugural National Women's Soccer League (NWSL) with Portland Thorns in 2013 and a treble at Lyon four years later.

> '**You can tell why she's the best in the world... She loves detail. She wants to be challenged. She wants to get better every day.**'
>
> Orlando Pride coach Marc Skinner

HIGHLIGHTS

2008
Morgan scores four goals at the U20 World Cup and in doing so receives the Bronze Boot, as well as the Silver Ball for being the second best player of the tournament.

2011
Morgan leaves the University of California, Berkeley after scoring 45 goals in four years and is drafted by the Western New York Flash.

2011
Morgan comes on as a substitute in a key World Cup qualifier against Italy and scores to give USA an advantage and later qualify for the tournament. At the tournament she becomes the first player to score a goal and register an assist in a World Cup final.

2012
Morgan scores 28 goals and adds 21 assists and becomes only the second American, after Mia Hamm, to score 20-plus goals and register 20-plus assists in the same calendar year. Three of those come at the Summer Olympics as USA win a fourth Olympic gold.

FACT FILE

DOB: 02.07.89

HEIGHT: 1.70m (5'7")

WEIGHT: 62kg (137lb)

USA: Caps **169**
Goals **107**

POSITION: Forward

CLUBS: Olympique Lyonnais (current – loan), West Coast FC, California Storm, Pali Blues, Western New York Flash, Seattle Sounders Women, Portland Thorns, Orlando Pride

2013

Morgan joins Portland Thorns and helps the team win the league title in her first season.

2015

Morgan becomes a world champion and plays in all seven games, scoring against Colombia, as USA win their first World Cup since 1999.

2019

Two years after winning a treble with French side Olympique Lyonnais, she returns to France for the World Cup. She scores six goals, including five in one match and another on her birthday. She's awarded the Silver Boot.

DID YOU KNOW?

When she was seven, Morgan left a Post-It note in her mother's office saying she wanted to be 'a professional athlete for soccer' when she grew up.

KYLIAN
MBAPPÉ

Ask someone to choose the best footballer in the world and the chances are they'll decide between Lionel Messi and Cristiano Ronaldo. Yet there's a new challenger looking to break the duopoly. Kylian Mbappé is the most expensive teenager in world football, the second most expensive player ever behind club teammate Neymar, and he's already won the World Cup. He even scored in the final, becoming only the second teenager – after Pelé – to do so. Mbappé joined Paris Saint-Germain for €180m in 2018 and in less than three seasons he's amassed almost 80 goals. At the time of writing, he'd scored 19 times in 30 Champions League games, which is more than anyone else at his age in the competition. He's won three Ligue 1 titles and two cups in France. He's 21, he's quite good, and he has the potential to be the best of them all.

> '*Kylian has much more talent than I have. Do you see what he is doing at his age? No, I never had his talent.*'
> France teammate Paul Pogba

HIGHLIGHTS

2015
Mbappé makes his professional debut for Monaco, aged just 16 years and 347 days and in doing, becomes the club's youngest ever player. He scores his first goal in February 2016.

2017
Mbappé's breakthrough year brings records and silverware aplenty! He becomes the youngest player to score a hat-trick in Ligue 1, the second youngest French scorer in Champions League history and the youngest player in 30 years to score 10-plus league goals.

2017
Mbappé ends the 2016/17 season with a French league title and 26 goals in 44 appearances. Monaco finish as runners-up in the Couple de la Ligue and Trophée des Champions.

2017
His form earns him a record move to Paris Saint-Germain. He joins the Parisiens for €180m to make him the most expensive teenager in history.

FACT FILE

DOB: 20.12.98

HEIGHT: 1.78m (5'10")

WEIGHT: 73kg (161lb)

FRANCE: Caps **34** Goals **13**

POSITION: Forward

CLUBS: Paris Saint-Germain (current), Monaco

2018
He ends his first season with a treble consisting of the league title, French Cup and league cup. A year later he wins the league again, adds the Trophée des Champions to his collection, but misses out on the French Cup.

2018
Called up to France's World Cup squad. 'Les Bleus' go all the way to lift the trophy. He scores in a game against Peru to become the youngest scorer at the competition aged 19, then scored in the final. He wins the FIFA World Cup Best Young Player award.

2019
Aged 20 years and 306 days he becomes the youngest player to score 15-plus goals in the Champions League and then scores his 100th career goal, in a 4–0 win for France against Andorra.

DID YOU KNOW?
In 2018, Mbappe donated his World Cup fees to charity.
In 2020, Mbappé set up his own charity called Inspired by KM, set up to help kids aged between nine and 14 to achieve their dreams.

LIONEL
MESSI

Put simply, Lionel Messi is the best player in the world, and arguably the best of all time. Even in 2019, a year in which his country was disappointed at the Copa América, and his club squandered a three-goal lead to lose in the Champions League semi-final against Liverpool, Messi smashed more records than we have space to list here. He also surpassed 600 goals for Barcelona, won a record 10th La Liga title and a record sixth Golden Shoe. He was also the top scorer in Europe and the Champions League. Since 2010, he has scored 50 or more goals in nine out of 10 seasons, 579 in total. And he doesn't just score goals; he makes them too. Describing himself as a 'constructor', he's provided 230 career assists, more than anyone else. The king of all football.

'He is the best player I have ever seen. The best thing about him is not what he does but how simple he makes everything look.'

Former Barcelona coach Pep Guardiola

HIGHLIGHTS

2004
Messi joins Barcelona aged 13 and makes his competitive debut in October 2004.

2005
Messi wins the World Youth Championship and finishes the tournament with the Golden Ball for being the best player, and the Golden Shoe for most goals scored. A year later he becomes Argentina's youngest player and scorer at a World Cup. In 2008, he wins Olympic Gold in Beijing.

2009
He wins his first treble as a Barcelona player aged 22 and then caps a fine year by winning the first of six Ballon d'Or awards.

2012
Messi breaks the record for most goals scored in a single season in 2011/12 in both La Liga and Champions League and in doing so, becomes Barcelona's all-time record scorer. He wins an unprecedented fourth and consecutive Ballon d'Or.

FACT FILE

DOB: 24.06.87

HEIGHT: 1.70m (5'7")

WEIGHT: 72kg (159lb)

ARGENTINA: Caps **138**
Goals **70**

POSITION: Forward

CLUBS: Barcelona (current)

2014
Having now spent three years as captain, he leads Argentina to the World Cup final where they're beaten by Germany. He wins the Golden Ball for best player.

2015
Messi becomes the top scorer in La Liga history as he fires Barça to another treble, before winning the Ballon d'Or a fifth time.

2018
Messi is given the Barcelona captaincy. A year later he wins his sixth Ballon d'Or award.

DID YOU KNOW?
Messi has won more Ballon d'Or awards (six), more Golden Shoes (six) and more trophies (34) than anyone else ever.

NEYMAR

While 2019 wasn't a vintage year for Neymar da Silva Santos Júnior, usually known simply as Neymar, he still managed to pick up a league winners' medal with Paris Saint-Germain (PSG), his second since joining the club in 2017, and his fifth winners' medal in total in France. Neymar was injured as Brazil cruised to victory in the Copa América on home soil, and the uncertainty about his future, with talk with a move away from Paris, that encapsulated a disappointing 12 months. Despite rumours of a move back to Barcelona, he returned to his best form in December, when he scored every time he played and contributed to eight goals. He had 13 shots on target, more than any other player in Ligue 1, and completed 19 dribbles, the second highest of any player in the French top flight.

> *'Neymar is a phenomenon. It's nice to see a Brazilian continuing to make history and I think he can be the greatest in the world.'*
>
> Brazil legend Ronaldinho

HIGHLIGHTS

2009
Neymar makes his professional debut aged 17 for Santos. He helps the club win consecutive league titles, in 2010, 2011 and 2012, the Brazil Cup in 2010 and a first Copa Libertadores title since 1963 in 2011.

2011
He wins the South American Footballer of the Year award for the first time – and again a year later.

2013
The Brazilian joins Barcelona, where he wins the Supercopa de España in his first year and consecutive league titles in 2015 and 2016. By the time he joins PSG in 2017, he's won eight trophies in Spain.

2016
Neymar captains Brazil to gold at the Summer Olympics on home soil in Rio.

2018

His first year in
France is a profitable
one as PSG win Ligue
1 plus three cups:
the French Cup, the
French league Cup
and the Trophée des
Champions. He's
announced as the
Ligue 1 Player of
the Year.

2019

His goal for Brazil
against Colombia in
2019 takes his tally
to 61 in the famous
yellow jersey. He
plays his 100th match
for Brazil in October.

2020

By March Neymar
had scored seven
goals in nine
games. The start
of this completed a
sequence of scoring
in eight games in
a row, and took
his tally to 15 in all
competitions.

DID YOU KNOW?

Aged 27 and with time
on his side, Neymar
is already the third
highest goalscorer in
Brazil's history and
is primed to overtake
Ronaldo to close in on
top spot behind Pelé.

MANUEL
NEUER

While goalkeepers such as Ederson, Jan Oblak, Marc-André ter Stegen and Alisson Becker grab the headlines, legendary stopper Manuel Neuer continues to go about his business with the quality

'He's the best keeper in the world, has won lots of titles and is a World Champion! What more can he do?'

Former teammate Franck Ribéry

and consistency that have made him one of the world's best for over a decade. Yet as he approaches his mid-30s he faces fresh threats to the No. 1 jersey for both club and country. For Germany, he battles Barcelona starter Ter Stegen for a place, although in 2019 Neuer made his 37th clean sheet on international duty, a record. At club level, Neuer will soon have competition from 23-year-old stopper and new Bayern signing, Alexander Nübel. Nübel might be the future, but don't expect Neuer to wave the white flag anytime soon; in 2019 he was still making jaw-dropping saves with impressive regularity.

HIGHLIGHTS

2008
After signing professional forms at Schalke, Neuer plays every minute of the 2017/18 season – making 50 appearances in total – and is the youngest and only German-based player to be shortlisted for the Goalkeeper of the Year award.

2011
Now Schalke captain, Neuer lifts the DFB-Pokal cup and leads the side to the semi-finals of the Champions League for the first time. He joins Bayern Munich that summer.

2011
In his first season, Neuer breaks the record for most competitive clean sheets in a row after going more than 1,000 minutes without conceding a goal.

2013
Neuer and Bayern win the Champions League. Neuer makes eight saves in the final against Borussia Dortmund. They go on to win the UEFA Super Cup and FIFA Club World Cup.

FACT FILE

DOB: 27.03.86

HEIGHT: 1.93m (6'4")

WEIGHT: 92kg (203lb)

GERMANY: Caps **92** Goals **0**

POSITION: Goalkeeper

CLUBS: Bayern Munich (current), Schalke 04

2015
A year after he's announced as the World Goalkeeper of the Year, he wins the German Footballer of the Year award, is voted into the UEFA team of the year and finishes third in the Ballon d'Or.

2017
Neuer is named as Bayern Munich's new club captain and captain of the German national team following the retirement of Philip Lahm.

2019
Neuer and Bayern win a seventh consecutive Bundesliga title before lifting the DFB-Pokal cup, Neuer's fifth with the club.

DID YOU KNOW?
Neuer did the voiceover for character Frank McCay in the German version of the 2013 Disney animation *Monsters University*.

JAN
OBLAK

The best goalkeeper in the world?
Alisson Becker (Liverpool),
Ederson (Manchester City)
and Marc-André ter Stegen
(Barcelona) might have something
to say about that, but Jan Oblak
has been so consistent for so
long that he has every right to be
shortlisted. Crowned the best

*'Oblak is the best
goalkeeper in the world,
no doubt about it. He
continues to improve and
evolve every year, and he
helps the team to shine.'*
Atlético Madrid boss Diego Simeone

goalkeeper in Spain four years in a row, it took the tall Slovenian just 178
matches to register his 100th clean sheet at Atlético. Oblak honed his
skills watching his father Matjaž in action in Slovenia's third division. He'd
then cycle 40 miles (64km) a day to train. His efforts paid off. He made his
professional debut aged 16 and joined Portuguese giants Benfica aged 17.
Since joining Atlético in 2014, he has won three trophies and has kept a
clean sheet against every side he's faced in Spain, except Barcelona.

HIGHLIGHTS

2009
Oblak starts the
2009/10 season with
Olimpia Ljubljana
after rejecting Italian
side Empoli and an
unsuccessful trial at
Fulham. He makes
his debut aged 16 and
misses just
three games.

2010
Joins Benfica and
makes his league
debut two years
later. He makes
his mark in the
2013/14 campaign.
In 2012 he makes
his international
senior debut, against
Norway in a World
Cup qualifier.

2014
Wins Portugal's
Best Goalkeeper
of the Year award
before leaving for
Atlético Madrid
for €16m, which
made him the then
most expensive
goalkeeper in La
Liga history.

2015
Makes his mark
after coming on as
a substitute against
Bayer 04 Leverkusen in
the Champions League.
He saves a penalty in a
shootout and keeps the
No. 1 jersey from that
point. He becomes the
first-choice goalkeeper
for Slovenia.

FACT FILE

DOB: 07.01.93

HEIGHT: 1.88m (6'2")

WEIGHT: 87kg (192lb)

SLOVENIA: Caps 26
Goals 0

POSITION: Goalkeeper

CLUBS: Atlético Madrid (current), Olimpija Ljubljana, Benfica, Beira-Mar (loan), Olhanense (loan), União de Leiria (loan), Rio Ave (loan)

2016

By the end of his second season, Oblak wins the first of four Ricardo Zamora trophies after having conceded just 18 goals in 38 games, equalling a 22-year-old record.

2018

Wins a Europa League winners' medal, his first title with Atlético, after keeping a clean sheet against Olympique de Marseille.

2019

Oblak wins his fourth consecutive Ricardo Zamora trophy, equalling legendary goalkeeper Victor Valdés for most won in a row. In September, he is given the Slovenia captaincy.

DID YOU KNOW?

Oblak's older sister Teja has played professional basketball for Slovenia.

ALEXANDRA
POPP

Germany captain Alex Popp is a powerful player for club and country, a striker who averages a goal every two games no matter whom she's playing for. It's also no coincidence that wherever Popp goes, silverware tends to follow. In three years at FCR 2001 Dulsburg, her first professional club, she won a league title, consecutive German cups and the Champions League. She moved to Wolfsburg and won a treble in her first season, lifting the Frauen-Bundesliga title, the DFB-Pokal Frauen cup and the Champions League title. A year later, Popp scored the winning goal to secure a second consecutive league title as Wolfsburg dominated at home and abroad. As Wolfsburg look favourites to land another league title in 2020, she's already won five league titles, six German cups and two Champions League titles in seven years.

'I am very mentally strong... the ideal link between the team and the coaching team.'
Alexandra Popp

HIGHLIGHTS

2009
Popp ends her first season at Duisburg by winning both the Women's Champions League and German Cup. She's also awarded the Fritz Walter Medal as the best female junior player that year.

2010
More silverware follows as Popp wins the German cup once again. She also wins an U20 World Cup winners' medal with Germany. She scores in every game, 10 goals in total, and wins the Golden Ball and Golden Shoe.

2011
At the World Cup, she scores four goals in one game, only the seventh German female player to do so, in a 17–0 win against Kazakhstan.

2012
Popp joins Wolfsburg and in her first season helps the side win a treble consisting of the league title, the DFB-Pokal Frauen and Champions League.

FACT FILE

DOB: 06.04.91

HEIGHT: 1.75m (5'9")

WEIGHT: 65kg (143lb)

GERMANY: Caps **106** Goals **53**

POSITION: Forward

CLUBS: VfL Wolfsburg (current), FFC Recklinghausen, FCR 2001 Duisburg

2013
A year later, the league title comes down to the last day of the season, and Popp scores the winning goal, against FFC Frankfurt.

2016
Popp wins a gold medal at the summer Olympics. She plays in all six games, scores once and weighs in with two assists.

2019
Popp wins her fifth Bundesliga title with Wolfsburg and adds the DFB-Pokal Frauen cup for good measure. She then captains Germany at the World Cup in France and makes her 100th appearance for the country.

DID YOU KNOW?
In 2019, Popp became the 26th player to play 100 games for the German national team.

87

MEGAN
RAPINOE

They say that the best players are the ones who can deliver when it matters most, and in Megan Rapinoe, USA have a player who thrives on the big stage. The World Cup in 2019 was a game-changing experience for the US skipper who was arguably the most important player as USA reclaimed the World Cup. She scored in every game she played to win the Golden Boot with six goals (Alex Morgan and Ellen White scored six too, but Rapinoe won it by virtue of playing less minutes) and won the Golden Ball for being the standout player of the tournament. Off the pitch, her press conferences and interviews made headlines all over the world. She capped a fine year by being named Ballon d'Or winner later in December.

'Putting yourself out there is hard, but it's so worth it. I don't think anyone who has ever spoken out, or stood up or had a brave moment, has regretted it.'
Megan Rapinoe

HIGHLIGHTS

2009
After graduating from the University of Portland she joins the Chicago Red Stars in the Women's Professional Soccer (WPS) league as it was known at that time. She was named in the league's all-star team in her first year.

2011
Rapinoe plays a key role as USA win the World Cup in 2011. Her biggest contribution was a pinpoint assist for Abby Wambach in the quarter-final win over Brazil, the latest goal ever recorded in a World Cup game.

2012
Rapinoe scores three goals and contributes a team high of four assists at the London Olympics in 2012 as USA win gold. Of her three goals, she scores directly from a corner, the first footballer – male or female – to do so at the Olympics.

2012
She joined Seattle Sounders Women and helped the side sell out their 45,000-seater stadium in nine of their 10 matches that season.

FACT FILE

DOB: 05.07.1985

HEIGHT: 1.68m (5'6")

WEIGHT: 60kg (132lb)

USA: Caps 160 Goals 50

POSITION: Midfield

CLUBS: Reign FC (current), Chicago Red Stars, Philadelphia Independence, magicJack, Sydney FC, Seattle Sounders Women, Olympique Lyonnais

2013
Rapinoe joins Seattle Reign FC and despite playing just 12 out of 22 games, she finishes the side's highest scorer with five goals.

2014
After joining Olympique Lyonnais she helps the club reach the Champions League final, and becomes only the fifth American women to play in the final. They lose to Wolfsburg.

2019
She wins the Golden Ball and the Golden Boot at the World Cup in France, starring, and scoring six goals as USA win the competition for the second time in a row.

FAMOUS FOR…
Rapinoe is now arguably the most famous and recognisable player in women's football. Her pink pixie haircut and iconic goal celebration, with arms outstretched, were arguably the standout images of the 2019 World Cup.

WENDIE RENARD

Top clubs are built on solid foundations, and in captain Wendie Renard, Olympique Lyonnais have one of the best and most consistent central defenders in the game. A commanding player who gives little away on the floor or in the air thanks to her speed, physicality and technique, she's also a fairly formidable presence from set pieces at the opposite end of the field. She scored three goals at the World Cup – at which she was the tallest player – in 2019 and had netted eight goals in the current domestic campaign by mid-January 2020, including a hat-trick on Champions League duty, as she looks to win her 14th league title with Lyon. Since her first season as a pro at the club, in 2007/08, Renard has won the Champions League six times, as well as eight cups.

> *'I don't think there's anyone quite like her in the women's game.'*
> **Norway international Maren Mjelde**

HIGHLIGHTS

2006
After an unsuccessful trial at France's national training academy, aged 15, Renard hops on a train to try her luck at Olympique Lyonnais. She's more successful there, and she joins the club aged 16 in 2006.

2007
Renard wins the league title at the end of her first season, the first of 13 she's won at the club.

2011
Renard plays in her first Champions League final and scores the opening goal in a 2–0 win against Turbine Potsdam in the final. She has since won the competition a further five times.

2011
Renard makes her France debut against Switzerland in the Cyprus Cup. She later wins the competition in 2012 and 2014.

FACT FILE

DOB: 20.07.90

HEIGHT: 1.88m (6'2")

WEIGHT: 70kg (154lb)

FRANCE: Caps **118** Goals **23**

POSITION: Defence

CLUBS: Olympique Lyonnais (current)

2013

After making her France debut in 2011, she is given the captaincy two years later, in September.

2017

Renard wins her first tournament with France, the SheBelieves Cup. In the same year, France are beaten in the European Championship quarter-finals, against England.

2019

Renard has a mixed World Cup, scoring three goals including two against South Korea, but an own goal against Norway. France lose to eventual winners USA in the quarter-finals.

DID YOU KNOW?

In January 2020, Renard accidentally left the suitcase containing both the 'FIFA the Best' and Ballon d'Or World XI awards on a train. At the time of writing, they still haven't been found.

CRISTIANO
RONALDO

New year, same old Cristiano Ronaldo ... the star kicked off 2020 by scoring yet more goals. He netted a hat-trick in the first game of the year, against Cagliari, and scored in 10 consecutive matches, to continue his remarkable record. Since 2010, he has averaged just over 48 goals a season at club level, his best year coming in 2013, when he scored 59 times for Real Madrid. In that time, he has scored 77 goals for Portugal, helping them win the European Championship (2016) and Nations League (2019). He has won six league winners' medals – is the only player to lift the league title in England, Spain and Italy – and the Champions League four times. He's been awarded the Ballon d'Or five times. Only Lionel Messi, his long-standing rival, has won it more (six times).

'This man is the best... Cristiano is a goals machine. He is an incredible player. There will never be another Ronaldo.'

Former Real Madrid coach José Mourinho

HIGHLIGHTS

2002
Makes a great impression in a friendly against Manchester United with first club Sporting Clube de Portugal, and moves to Old Trafford in 2003, aged 18.

2004
Wins the FA Cup in his first season, the first of many trophies to follow. The Premier League title comes in 2007, the first of three in a row, and then the Champions League in 2008.

2008
Wins the Champions League, and ends the season with 42 goals in all competitions, his best return for United. They then win the Club World Cup, and Ronaldo wins the Ballon d'Or for the first time.

2009
Ronaldo joins Real Madrid for a then world record fee of £80m. He wins his first trophy with the club, the Copa del Rey, in 2011. It's the first of 15 trophies in total.

FACT FILE

DOB: 05.02.85

HEIGHT: 1.88m (6'2")

WEIGHT: 84kg (185lb)

PORTUGAL: Caps **164**
Goals **99**

POSITION: Forward

CLUBS: Juventus
(current), Sporting Lisbon,
Manchester United,
Real Madrid

2015
Ronaldo is
named the best
Portuguese player
of all time by
the Portuguese
Football
Federation.

2016
Captain Ronaldo
leads Portugal
to their first ever
tournament win,
in Euro 2016. He
wins the Silver Boot
for finishing as
the competition's
second highest
goalscorer.

2018
Becomes the first player
to win the Ballon d'Or five
times, the first player
to win the Champions
League five times, and
joins Juventus for £88m.
He becomes the highest
European international
goalscorer of all time.

DID YOU KNOW?
Cristiano Ronaldo is
an incredible physical
specimen, and at the
end of 2019 he scored
a header against
Sampdoria that saw
him jump 2.56m (8'4")
high in the air.

MOHAMED SALAH

When Mohamed Salah joined Liverpool in 2017, few could have expected what was to follow in his debut season for the 'Redmen'. Before his move to Merseyside, he'd been rejected by Chelsea but averaged a goal every other game while at Italian club Roma, first on loan and then when his move was made permanent in 2016. In his first full season in Serie A, he helped the side finish second in the league with a record points tally. At Liverpool, however, everything he touched turned to gold … and ended up in the net. He scored 44 goals in all competitions, 32 of which came in 36 league games, a record for a 38-game campaign. He won the Golden Boot and was named PFA Player of the Year. He didn't quite match his record-breaking numbers in 2018/19 but still netted 27 times as Liverpool won the Champions League.

'He's in the middle of the dressing room, he's sensationally good with all the boys and he is very influential for us.'

Liverpool boss Jürgen Klopp

HIGHLIGHTS

2012
Salah heads to Europe from first club El Mokawloon Al Arab in Egypt, and joins Swiss side Basel in 2012.

2012
Despite his disappointing run of form at club level, he performs well for Egypt at the Olympic Games and is awarded the Most Promising African Talent of the Year for his performances.

2013
Salah finds goals difficult to come by in Switzerland but he forms part of a Basel side that wins the league title. He scores a modest nine goals in 47 games, but does enough to interest Chelsea, who sign him in 2014.

2015
Salah struggles for first-team football and joins Italian side Fiorentina on loan, then Roma. The latter sign him permanently in 2016, and he helps the Italian side finish second in Serie A with a record points tally.

2017
Salah joins Liverpool for a then club-record fee of £36.9m. He moves from the wing to the centre of attack ... and he breaks the Premier League scoring record in his first season.

2018
In 2017, Salah helps Egypt reach the final of the Africa Cup of Nations and top scores as they qualify for the 2018 World Cup. He's named the African Footballer of the Year for the first time.

2019
Named African Footballer of the Year for a second year running and finishes his second season at Merseyside as the club's highest goalscorer again with 27 goals.

DID YOU KNOW?
Salah's family was robbed during his time in Egypt. However, he persuaded his dad to drop the charges against the offender and instead helped the thief financially in an effort to try to find him a job.

BERNARDO
SILVA

The Portuguese attacking midfielder boasts a silky left foot and has become one of Manchester City's most important players. He can play on the right side and cut inside to make or score goals, just as he did with devastating effect when he found the top corner in the victory against Manchester United in the League Cup semi-final in January 2020. He can also dictate games from a central position, and it was behind Raheem Sterling and Sergio Agüero that Silva played a key role – playing more league games than anyone else – as City won the Premier League in 2018/19. He scored six goals and contributed eight assists, but also did plenty of dirty work to press the opposition too. In September 2019, Silva netted the first hat-trick of his career as City thrashed Watford 8-0, the joint second-biggest scoreline in Premier League history.

'Right now it's Bernardo and 10 more players.'

Manchester city boss Pep Guardiola

HIGHLIGHTS

2013
Silva impresses for Portugal's U19s at the U19 European Championship as they reach the semi-finals. He's later named among the top 10 talents under the age of 19.

2014
From Benfica's youth academy, Silva steps up to the club's B team in 2013 and was promoted to the first team in 2014. Benfica win La Liga, the Taça de Portugal and the Taça de Liga.

2015
The Portuguese midfielder joins French side Monaco, who win the French league title in 2017. He scores 11 goals and adds 12 assists.

2015
Silva scores against Germany in the semi-finals of the U21 European Championship but Portugal lose in the final to Sweden.

FACT FILE

DOB: 10.08.94

HEIGHT: 1.73m (5'8")

WEIGHT: 64kg (141lb)

PORTUGAL: Caps **42** Goals **6**

POSITION: Midfield

CLUBS: Manchester City (current), Benfica, Monaco

2017
Silva impresses City when playing against them for Monaco in the Champions League, and City sign him that summer. In his first season, he plays more matches than anyone else (53).

2019
Silva finishes his second season with another 51 appearances, 13 goals and 14 assists. He starts the 2019/20 season with a hat-trick in City's 8–0 thrashing of Watford and is on the shortlist for the Ballon d'Or.

2019
Silva plays both matches in the Nations League Finals as Portugal lift the trophy.

DID YOU KNOW?
Silva was voted best player at the UEFA Nations League Finals in 2019, in which Portugal won the tournament on home soil.

RAHEEM
STERLING

Sterling is currently one of the most influential players in English football on and off the pitch. The 2018/19 season was his most successful to date, the forward getting himself into scoring positions more often and adding clinical finishing to his trickery and pace to take his game to another

'He is so confident and has so much belief in himself. He is almost unplayable.'

BBC pundit Alan Shearer

level. After playing well at the 2018 World Cup and helping England reach the semi-finals for the first time in 28 years, he then scored 25 goals and provided 18 assists in 51 games as City won the Community Shield, Premier League, FA Cup and League Cup. Sterling also had to make space on his mantelpiece for the PFA Young Player of the Year and Football Writer's Association Footballer of the Year awards. By December 2019, though, he'd already scored 18 goals and was well on course to smash his personal best.

HIGHLIGHTS

2003
After impressing at local youth team Alpha & Omega, Sterling joins Queens Park Rangers.

2010
Seven years later he joins Rafa Benítez's Liverpool for an initial fee of just £600k.

2012
He makes his senior debut against Wigan Athletic aged 17 years and 107 days to become Liverpool's youngest ever player. He also makes his first senior international debut, against Sweden.

2014
After being shortlisted for the PFA Young Player of the Year award at the end of the 2013/14 season, he's named Liverpool's Young Player of the Year. In December he wins the Golden Boy award for the best young footballer for the calendar year of 2014.

FACT FILE

DOB: 08.12.94

HEIGHT: 1.70m (5'7")

WEIGHT: 69kg (152lb)

ENGLAND: Caps 67
Goals 12

POSITION: Forward

CLUBS: Manchester
City (current), Liverpool,
Queens Park Rangers,
Alpha & Omega

2015
Liverpool finish the
league in second
place, with Sterling
having formed an
impressive front three
with Luis Suárez and
Daniel Sturridge. Joins
Manchester City for
£44m, the highest
English fee of all time.

2018
Finishes his best
season to date
with 18 goals. A
year later he wins
a domestic treble.

2019
Nets his 50th Premier
League goal, his 50th
goal for City in all
competitions, and a hat-
trick in 13 minutes.
Wins the PFA Young
Player of the Year
and Football Writer's
Association Footballer of
the Year awards.

DID YOU KNOW?
Sterling won his first
England cap aged 17.
By the age of 24, he
had won two Premier
League winners'
medals.

MARC-ANDRÉ TER
STEGEN

We're currently living in a golden age of goalkeeping. In England and Spain in particular, there are a number of keepers at the peak of their powers, not just by keeping the ball out of the net but also by excelling with the ball at their feet. Barcelona keeper Marc-André ter Stegen can lay claim to being the best of them all. In fact, such is his influence that he is considered just as important to the 'Blaugrana' as striker Lionel Messi. Admittedly, the Argentine forward makes the headlines and wins the personal plaudits, but Ter Stegen makes winning saves in the biggest matches with moments of individual brilliance. He keeps Barcelona in games, which enables Messi to win them at the other end; his presence, shot-stopping ability and concentration levels are unrivalled.

'He's the best in the world. It's a pleasure to have Ter Stegen in the team. He always helps us. It's great to have him.'

Barcelona teammate Sergi Roberto

HIGHLIGHTS

2010
Ter Stegen joins his hometown club Borussia Mönchengladbach. In 2011, he gets his chance in the first team and keeps four clean sheets in five games to help them avoid relegation from the Bundesliga.

2012
In his second season, Ter Stegen stars once more as Gladbach mount a surprise title challenge.

2014
Ter Stegen joins Barcelona and in his first season stars as Barça win the Copa del Rey and Champions League. He also wins a La Liga winners' medal, the first of four.

2015
Ter Stegen adds the UEFA Super Cup and the FIFA World Club Cup to his collection.

FACT FILE

DOB: 30.04.92

HEIGHT: 1.88m (6'2")

WEIGHT: 85kg (187lb)

GERMAN: Caps **24** Goals **0**

POSITION: Goalkeeper

CLUBS: Barcelona (current), Borussia Mönchengladbach

2016
He becomes Barça's first-team goalkeeper in all competitions following teammate Claudio Bravo's transfer to Manchester City.

2019
Becomes the first goalkeeper this century to provide an assist in La Liga when he passes to Luis Suárez against Getafe. Marks his 200th game for Barça with a clean sheet.

2020
New year, same consistency. Ter Stegen remains at the top of his game, with incredible saves against Getafe and Napoli among his repertoire.

DID YOU KNOW?
Despite his brilliance, Ter Stegen isn't Germany's first-choice goalkeeper. Yet. He currently shares duties with compatriot Manuel Neuer.

VIRGIL
VAN DIJK

No one single player is ever greater than the sum of all the parts that make up a football team, but the signing of Virgil van Dijk took Liverpool to new heights. In 2019, the 'Reds' were crowned the best team in Europe and then the world, and in 2020 they looked set to be top dogs in England, and van Dijk has been the final part of the jigsaw. Unquestionably the best defender in the world, it's not just the Dutchman's power, pace, composure and reading of the game that sets him apart from the rest, it's also the calming effect he has on others around him. Van Dijk has everything. He's good on the ball, in the air, in the challenge. In 2019 he was named PFA Player of the Year, UEFA Men's Player of the Year and came second only to Lionel Messi for the Ballon d'Or.

'He's good, really good, outstandingly good – but he has to be (because) he's a very talented boy. He just has to use that talent and it would be a shame if he doesn't.'

Liverpool coach Jürgen Klopp

HIGHLIGHTS

2013
Van Dijk starts his career in Holland at Groningen before signing for Celtic in 2013. He wins the Scottish league title in his first season, and his second, and is named in the PFA Scotland Team of the Year both times.

2015
After adding a Scottish Cup to his collection, van Dijk leaves Scotland for Southampton.

2017
Van Dijk is given the captain's armband following the departure of José Fonte. Later that year, he hands in a transfer request stating his wish to join Liverpool. He finally joins the Merseysiders in January 2018 for an undisclosed record fee.

2018
He scores on his debut against rivals Everton in an FA Cup tie and becomes the first player since Billy White to score on his debut in the Merseyside derby.

FACT FILE

DOB: 08.07.91

HEIGHT: 1.93m (6'4")

WEIGHT: 92kg (203lb)

NETHERLANDS: Caps **33**
Goals **4**

POSITION: Defender

CLUBS: Liverpool
(current), Groningen,
Celtic, Southampton

2018
Van Dijk is
awarded the
Netherlands
captaincy by
manager Ronald
Koeman.

2019
Van Dijk takes his
game to another
level and finishes the
2018/19 season the
PFA Player of the Year
and a Champions
League winner after
Liverpool defeat Spurs
in the final in Madrid.
Van Dijk is named man
of the match.

2019
Van Dijk wins the
UEFA Player of the
Year award and is
shortlisted for the
Ballon d'Or. He wins
the Club World Cup
after Liverpool beat
Flamengo in the final.

DID YOU KNOW?
Aged 20, van Dijk was
struggling to make the
Groningen first team,
and he would work
as a dishwasher two
nights a week to help
make ends meet.

DANIËLLE
VAN DE DONK

On the surface, Arsenal's WSL victory in 2018/19 looked to be the result of Vivianne Miedema's incredible run in front of goal, in which she netted 22 goals. However, behind the Dutch striker were a number of creative players who pitched in with goals and provided crucial creativity. Jordan Nobbs scored nine goals, Kim Little eight, while Daniëlle van de Donk weighed in with 11 of her own – often in crucial matches – and made six assists. Her form continued into the new season, with eight goals, three assists, and Arsenal challenging at the top of the league heading into March. Van de Donk is an intelligent player who finds space between the lines to gain an advantage over her opponents.

> *'Daniëlle is a very talented and skilful player... She brings a world-class attitude and quality that are vital to our team.'*
> Arsenal coach Joe Montemurro

HIGHLIGHTS

2010
Van de Donk makes her senior debut for Netherlands against Mexico right at the start of her career. She waits a further three years for her first international goal.

2012
Leaves first club, Willem II, to join VVV-Venlo in 2011. In her first season, she scores eight goals in 18 games and reaches the KNVB Women's Cup final, which Venlo lose, before joining PSV/FC Eindhoven.

2013
Van de Donk enjoys her best season in terms of goals, netting 14 goals at the end of her first season.

2015
In two seasons with Eindhoven, Van de Donk scores an impressive 30 goals in 53 appearances but only has a KNVB Women's Cup runners-up medal to show for her efforts.

FACT FILE

DOB: 05.08.91

HEIGHT: 1.60m (5'3")

WEIGHT: 54kg (119lb)

NETHERLANDS: Caps
102 Goals **21**

POSITION: Midfield

CLUBS: Arsenal (current),
Willem II, VVV Venlo,
PSV/FC Eindhoven,
Koppabergs/Göteborg

2015
The Dutch player joins Arsenal and she plays in the FA Women's Cup final at the end of her first season, beating Chelsea as Arsenal win a 14th FA Cup title.

2017
Van de Donk is an important part of the Netherlands side that wins the 2017 European Championship and she impresses in the final, against Denmark.

2019
Van de Donk stars with 11 goals in 19 league games as Arsenal win the FA Women's Super League. In October that year, she makes her 100th appearance for the Netherlands, against Russia.

DID YOU KNOW?
Van de Donk won a European Championship winners' medal in 2017 on home soil.

SARI
VAN VEENENDAAL

2019 was a strange 12 months for Dutch goalkeeper Sari van Veenendaal. She spent much of the first half of the year watching from the sidelines as Arsenal

'I want to be the best Sari that I can be.'
Van Veenendaal

won a first league title for seven years, but she ended it having played – and starred – in a World Cup, reaching the final, and as a regular in Spain following a move to Atlético Madrid. Van Veenendaal conceded just five goals at the World Cup and she played an important role as Netherlands overcame Japan and Sweden to reach the final, where she kept USA at bay with a string of saves … until she was beaten from the penalty spot. Despite the loss, she was named player of the match and won the tournament's Golden Glove award for best keeper. In 2017, she played all six games and conceded just three goals in six games as Netherlands won the UEFA European Championship.

HIGHLIGHTS

2007
A young Van Veenendaal takes her first steps in the game with Dutch side FC Utrecht, but she plays just two games as an understudy to the more established Angela Christ.

2010
Joins another Dutch side FC Twente in search of first-team football and wins the Eredivisie in her first season. She wins further league titles, the BeNe League as it was known, in 2013, 2014 and 2015.

2011
Wins her first international cap – and keeps a clean sheet – in a 6–0 win against Switzerland in the Cyprus Cup.

2015
On the move again, this time to London, where Van Veenendaal joins Arsenal. She wins the Women's FA Cup in her first year with the Gunners.

FACT FILE

DOB: 03.04.90

HEIGHT: 1.78m (5'10")

WEIGHT: 72kg (159lb)

NETHERLANDS: Caps **64** Goals **0**

POSITION: Goalkeeper

CLUBS: Atlético Madrid (current), FC Utrecht, FC Twente, Arsenal

2017
Van Veenendaal starts all six games as Netherlands lift the European Championship. She is named in the Best XI of the tournament.

2018
Wins a second FA Cup winners' medal but has to share goalkeeping duties with French teammate Pauline Peyraud-Magnin.

2019
Despite not being a first-team regular at Arsenal, is named as FIFA's best female goalkeeper in the world. She is one of the stars of the 2019 World Cup as Netherlands reach the final.

DID YOU KNOW?
Van Veenendaal is a winner. She won four league titles in five years during her time at FC Twente, then lifted a cup in three of her four seasons at Arsenal.

ELLEN WHITE

Ellen White came so close to top scoring at the World Cup in 2019. She finished the tournament with six goals, the same number as US duo Megan Rapinoe and Alex Morgan, but had two goals disallowed. The

'To make that unbelievable rise to where she was the best centre-forward in the [World Cup] tournament, is a credit to her professionalism, dedication and her desire to do well.'

England coach Phil Neville

first of these came in the semi-final against USA at a crucial point of the game, with England a goal behind. Had the goal stood, the outcome might have been different. We'll never know! What we do know is that when fit, White is prolific in front of goal, and she's improved her game by spending more time in the 18-yard box. After returning to action from injury at the start of the 2019/20 season, she scored eight goals in 14 starts for City as they attempted to topple Arsenal in the Women's Super League (WSL).

HIGHLIGHTS

2005
After spells at Aylesbury Town and Arsenal Ladies as a youngster, White leaves the Gunners aged 16 to join London rivals Chelsea. With 21 goals in 48 games, White top scores in each of her three seasons.

2008
Joins Leeds Carnegie but picks up a nasty injury that leaves her sidelined. By 2010 she has returned to her goalscoring best and scores twice as Leeds beat Everton in the final to lift the Premier League Cup.

2010
Rejoins Arsenal after a break of five years. She wins the FA Women's Super League in 2011 alongside the Women's FA Cup and WSL Cup in a glory-laden first season.

2011
White is voted England Women's Player of the Year. She scores a wonder goal against Japan at the World Cup in Germany, the team that go on to lift the title.

FACT FILE

DOB: 09.05.89

HEIGHT: 1.70m (5'7")

WEIGHT: 58kg (128lb)

ENGLAND: Caps **89** Goals **35**

POSITION: Forward

CLUBS: Manchester City (current), Chelsea, Leeds Carnegie, Arsenal, Notts County, Birmingham City

2013
White wins a cup double in her third season, lifting the WSL Cup for the third season in a row.

2019
Before joining Manchester City, White has spells at Notts County and Birmingham City. She reaches the 2017 Women's FA Cup final in 2017 after scoring the winning penalty in a shootout.

2019
Becomes England's all-time top World Cup scorer. At the time of writing, she's amassed 35 goals in 89 games and is England's fifth highest scorer ever, 12 shy of becoming the Lioness' all-time top scorer.

FAMOUS FOR...
Her 'goggles' celebration is a tribute to Cologne striker Anthony Modeste, who celebrates the same way, and of whom she is a big fan!

FOOTBALL STARS
30 UNDER 30

Picking the world's best 50 players was hard, but identifying the cream of the crop of those up-and-coming footballers, aged younger than 30 was even harder; there are so many good young players around! From great goalkeepers to sensational strikers, here's our pick of the best rising stars and those who are already household names.

AITANA BONMATÍ

A three-time runner-up with Barcelona in Spain's Primera División de la Liga de Fútbol Femenino in consecutive seasons, Aitana Bonmatí finally looked set to finish first. The talented, creative midfielder scored five goals in nine games to help lift Barça above rivals Atlético Madrid in the 2019/20 season. She can play in the centre of midfield or on the wing – and she loves to attack. Should Barça win the league, her next target will no doubt be victory in the Champions League after the 'Blaugrana' finished runners-up in 2019. Now a full international with Spain, she'll be looking to Women's Euro 2021 to replicate the European success she enjoyed at U17 and U19 levels.

> DID YOU KNOW: In 2019, Bonmati was rewarded for her superb performances for Barcelona, which she joined aged 14, with the Catalan Women's Player of the Year award.

ELLIE CARPENTER

Still under 21 and already a regular for club and country, Carpenter is a fearless defender who represents a new breed of attacking full-backs, and who has the potential to become a big star. Carpenter is full of energy and always performs with the same all-or-nothing intensity. In 2018, she joined National Women's Soccer League (NWSL) side Portland Thorns and quickly became the division's youngest ever player aged 18 years and 11 days, and youngest goalscorer weeks later. Two years earlier, in 2016, she was Australia's youngest Olympian at the Rio Games. Expect Carpenter to keep breaking boundaries.

DID YOU KNOW: When Carpenter started for the 'Matildas' against Vietnam in 2016 aged just 15, she became Australia's first international footballer born in the 21st century.

SARA DÄBRITZ

The technically excellent midfielder was Germany's standout player at the 2019 World Cup in France. She scored three goals, won two player-of-the-match awards and was generally playing at her peak before she was cruelly sidelined after injuring her anterior cruciate ligament. The World Cup had followed a fine campaign for Däbritz at Bayern Munich. Combining vision with clinical finishing, she scored 13 goals and added nine assists. Unfortunately, it wasn't enough to topple the mighty VfL Wolfsburg, or for Däbritz to add a second league winners' medal to the one she won in 2016, but she moved to Paris Saint-Germain in 2019 eager to grow her trophy collection.

DID YOU KNOW: Däbritz is an Olympic gold medallist, a European champion, an U20 world champion and an U17 European champion.

MATTHIJS DE LIGT

Juventus took decisive action after losing to Ajax in the Champions League quarter-finals in 2018/19 … by signing one of the players who had contributed to their elimination. Defender Matthijs de Ligt scored against the 'Bianconeri' with a trademark towering header, and then kept Juve's attackers at bay, which cumulatively prompted his €75m move. The Dutchman faces stiff competition for places in Turin with Juve boasting an embarrassment of riches in that position, but boss Maurizio Sarri believes de Ligt can 'become the best defender in the world'. He has extraordinary leadership skills that belie his age, he is an excellent reader of the game, and he can play out from the back.

DID YOU KNOW: De Ligt was a huge Ajax fan who watched them win four consecutive league titles. Then, as a player, he lifted the title as captain when they won it in 2019.

FRENKIE DE JONG

Barcelona are rebuilding their midfield following the departures of legends Andrés Iniesta and Xavi, but in Frenkie de Jong they have a top talent. Still only 22, de Jong is one of Europe's brightest stars and though he's still finding his feet at Camp Nou, his vision and inch-perfect passing are well matched with the style of the 'Blaugrana'. Spanish fans had been given a taste of his talents when he dominated for Ajax against Real Madrid in the Champions League last 16, second leg in 2018/19. De Jong was imperious as Ajax came from behind to stun Real 4–1 at the Bernabéu Stadium. He shone again, against Juventus in the quarter-finals.

DID YOU KNOW: In his last season at Dutch side Ajax, de Jong boasted a staggering passing accuracy of 91.4 per cent. That's a whole season of rarely giving the ball away.

FABINHO

Liverpool took their consistency to another level in 2019/20 and it was players such as Fabinho, shielding the defence, who gifted the attacking players with the freedom to unleash mayhem at the other end of the pitch. The Brazilian had struggled to hold down a regular place after joining the club in 2018 from Monaco, but his progress in 2019 was incredible. Now, Liverpool boss Jürgen Klopp describes him as an 'incredibly important' player, and he could be considered the best defensive midfielder around, such has been his consistency. His impact on the side is huge but subtle, the athletic 26-year-old winning possession and launching attacks with incredible efficiency and elegance.

DID YOU KNOW: Fábio Henrique Tavares, aka Fabinho, was persuaded to join Liverpool by Brazilian teammate Roberto Firmino when the two were on international duty.

JOÃO FÉLIX

It's a big year for the gifted João Félix, who after joining Atlético Madrid for a whopping £113m – he's the second most expensive teenager behind Kylian Mbappé – is yet to replicate the dazzling trickery and goalscoring form that tempted the Spanish club to sign him from Benfica. Atlético boss Diego Simeone is still finding Félix's best position, though he saw signs of his brilliance in pre-season when Félix scored twice against Juventus and again against Real Madrid. He was awarded the Golden Boy award as Europe's best young player in 2019 and, at Atlético, who have an alumni of talented strikers he's at the best place to hone his goalscoring talents.

DID YOU KNOW: By netting three times against Eintracht Frankfurt in April 2019, Félix became the youngest ever player to score a hat-trick in the Europa League (aged 19 years and 152 days).

SERGE GNABRY

Football really is a funny old game. After signing for Arsenal as a teenager, Gnabry joined West Bromwich Albion on loan in 2015/16 to get more games. However, he was recalled midway through that season because he wasn't playing. Five years on, Gnabry is a world star. His remarkable turnaround began at German club Werder Bremen, where he scored 11 goals in 27 games before joining Bayern Munich in 2017. He went out on loan once more, this time to Hoffenheim, where he averaged a goal every two games. Then, in 2018/19 he scored Bayern's 4,000th goal in the Bundesliga, one of 10 goals in 30 games that helped them win the league title, and was named Player of the Year.

DID YOU KNOW: In October 2019, Gnabry scored four goals in 35 minutes as Bayern Munich defeated Tottenham Hotspur 7–2 in the Champions League.

CAROLINE GRAHAM HANSEN

Creative midfielder Caroline Graham Hansen had already achieved a lot in the game before she signed for ambitious Spanish side Barcelona in 2019. She won a Frauen Bundesliga winner's medal in her final season at German club VfL Wolfsburg – her third German title in as many years – before becoming the first Norwegian female to play in Spain. Her six goals and seven assists at the midway point of the 2019/20 campaign gave Barcelona breathing space at the top of the Primera División. For Norway, she netted 11 goals in her last five internationals, including two hat-tricks, and she was the country's best player at the World Cup in 2019 as they reached the quarter-finals.

DID YOU KNOW: Want an assist? Graham Hansen's passing and vision are what you need. In 2019, she contributed 30 while on duty for VfL Wolfsburg, Norway and Barcelona.

JACKIE GROENEN

When Jackie Groenen joined Manchester United in the summer of 2019, the Dutch midfielder was hoping the move would prove more successful than her first stint in England. Groenen had a relatively disappointing 18-month spell at Chelsea from 2014, but a lot has happened since then. First, she was part of the Netherlands team that won the European Championship on home soil in 2017, then she starred in the semi-final of the World Cup in 2019, scoring the winning goal against Sweden, as the Dutch came close to winning a second successive major tournament. Groenen joined the recently promoted United as a marquee signing, and she hasn't disappointed.

DID YOU KNOW: As a teenager, Groenen was a Dutch judo champion. She won a European bronze aged 15, and continued as a judoka until she was 17.

ERLING BRAUT HAALAND

It's fair to say that striker Erling Braut Haaland was enjoying himself during the 2019/20 season. By the end of 2019 he had scored 24 goals and disappointed a whole host of clubs by signing for Borussia Dortmund in the January 2020 transfer window. After joining Austrian club Red Bull Salzburg from Norwegians Molde in January 2019, the young striker had started his first full season with a hot streak in front of goal that didn't stop. He netted 11 times in his first seven games and then struck a hat-trick on his Champions League debut, against Genk. He was the first player to score three times in his first Champions League game since Wayne Rooney in 2004.

DID YOU KNOW: In May 2019, Haaland broke the world record for the number of goals scored in an U20 World Cup match when he netted nine times against Honduras.

ACHRAF HAKIMI

Achraf Hakimi is in the form of his life, which is why it came as no surprise when, in 2019, he was awarded the African Football Federation Young Player of the Year award for the second consecutive year. The Moroccan international is in the second year of a two-season loan spell at Borussia Dortmund from Real Madrid. In 2018/19, he scored his first goal for the club in September and a month later contributed three assists in one match, but it wasn't until 2019/20 that he thrived. His speed, range of passing and overall awareness could see him in Real Madrid's first team when he returns to Spain. That, or he'll seal a deserved move elsewhere.

DID YOU KNOW: In the first half of 2019/20, Hakimi scored four goals in six Champions League matches – more than any other defender in the competition.

KAI HAVERTZ

Havertz might already be a Bundesliga centurion, but it's the quality as well as quantity that makes the midfielder such a star. Boasting incredible technical ability and decision-making in the final third, plus a potent goal threat, Havertz has broken all sorts of records. He became Bayer Leverkusen's youngster ever player in October 2016 when he made his debut aged 17 years, four months and five days. Seven months later, he became the club's youngster scorer when he netted an equaliser in a 3–3 draw against VfL Wolfsburg. He finished his first season with four goals and six assists in 24 appearances. In 2018/19, he netted 17 goals, the most by any teenager in Bundesliga history.

DID YOU KNOW: Only three players have amassed 100 Bundesliga appearances before their 21st birthday. Havertz is the youngest to do so, aged 20 years, six months and four days.

LINDSEY HORAN

Horan continues to set a high standard for club and country. In 2018, she was named Most Valuable Player (MVP) in the National Women's Soccer League (NWSL) after scoring 13 goals from midfield for Portland Thorns. She starred – and scored – in the play-offs against Seattle Reign, but couldn't quite do enough to help the club retain the league title. She also scored four goals as USA went the calendar year unbeaten. In 2019, though she didn't play every game at the World Cup in France, she made an impact when selected. She scored in a group win against Thailand and then starred as USA beat rivals England in the semi-finals, setting up Alex Morgan for the all-important second goal.

DID YOU KNOW: In 2019, Horan scored less than three minutes into the final World Cup group game, against rivals Sweden, to net the fastest goal of the tournament.

JOSHUA KIMMICH

'He's got absolutely everything', was how former Bayern Munich boss Pep Guardiola described a player who rarely delivers a bad performance wherever he's asked to play, whether it's for Bayern Munich – for whom he played every minute in their title-winning season in 2018/19 – or Germany. During his four-year career at Bayern he has played at right-back, centre back and in the No. 6 role in central midfield. It says much about his ability that he's considered pretty good in all three positions. He's still young and already has four Bundesliga winners' medals and 50 German caps. In 2019, he wore the captain's armband for Germany for the first time.

DID YOU KNOW: Kimmich was born in Rottweil, a medieval town in Germany famous for spawning the rottweiler, originally a breed of butcher's dog.

AYMERIC LAPORTE

Sometimes you don't know what you've got until it's gone, and that's been the case for Manchester City and centre-back Aymeric Laporte. After he suffered a serious knee injury in August 2019, Pep Guardiola's side started leaking goals. Laporte's absence left City vulnerable, particularly against teams they'd usually expect to beat. Laporte is world class, as shown during the 2018/19 season when he starred as City became the first team to hold all four of England's domestic trophies. Confident on the ball and prepared to do whatever it takes to prevent opponents from scoring, he has certainly been a valuable addition since his arrival from Athletic Bilbao in January 2018.

DID YOU KNOW: Laporte's father used to play rugby in the French second division. Laporte himself preferred to play football and so left home aged just 11 to attend a sports school.

AMEL MAJRI

The Olympique Lyonnais squad is full of stars, but for every Ada Hegerberg or Dzsenifer Marozsán there's an Amel Majri; a player who doesn't grab the headlines but who is a vital part of the equation. Majri can play either as a left-winger or left wing-back but wherever she starts, for club or country, she's a constant source of ammunition and inspiration. She's quick, loves to beat defenders and boasts a crossing ability that makes her very popular with her attacking teammates! She registered 14 goals and 12 assists in all competitions in 2018/19, then starred at the World Cup for France before registering six assists at the midway point of the new campaign.

DID YOU KNOW: Majri has an impressive honours list. She's won nine league titles, seven French cups and six Champions Leagues while with Olympique Lyonnais.

GRIEDGE MBOCK BATHY

Wendie Renard's place in our top 50 is assured, but it won't be long before her defensive partner Griedge Mbock surpasses her. Mbock has certainly been able to learn from one of the best in the business and she is now becoming the dominant half of a defensive duo that has proved an impenetrable wall for many opponents. In January 2020, the pair had kept clean sheets in 13 out of 15 games. Of course, Lyon tend to dominate games, which helps, but this just means that Mbock needs incredible levels of concentration to be able to do her job when needed. Calm with or without the ball and an excellent reader of the game, Mbock is reaching her peak.

DID YOU KNOW: Mbock has won every tournament available to her at club level, while with France she's won the U17 World Cup, U19 European Championship and 2017 SheBelieves Cup.

BETH MEAD

When Beth Mead scored a peach of a goal to help England beat Brazil at the SheBelieves Cup in 2019 it catapulted the Arsenal striker on to the world stage. Coming off the bench, Mead took the ball out of her feet with her first touch before unleashing a thunderous drive into the top corner from a tight angle. And it was no fluke, for she did it again a month later against Liverpool for Arsenal. Mead scored another goal at the SheBelieves Cup, against Japan, and then finished the 2018/19 campaign with 12 assists – more than any other player in the Women's Super League (WSL). At the World Cup she provided the most assists for England and has since scored in two of her last three internationals.

DID YOU KNOW: In 2015, Mead had a car accident that saw her flip her car while avoiding a deer. She emerged unscathed, and two days later scored a hat-trick for Sunderland against Chelsea.

MARTIN ØDEGAARD

Currently on loan at Spanish side Real Sociedad from Real Madrid, the 21-year-old has emerged as one of the best creative midfielders in La Liga, suggesting he could finally be given a chance at his parent club when he returns in the summer of 2020 (he joined Real Madrid in 2015). He came on as a sub to make his debut for 'Los Blancos' in 2014/15 aged just 16 years and 157 days, but he has had few opportunities since, instead impressing elsewhere. His best performance of the 2019/20 season came against Barcelona in December; he not only outshone his more experienced contemporaries, but he also had more shots and created more chances than anyone else on the pitch, including Lionel Messi.

DID YOU KNOW: When Ødegaard signed his first professional contract aged 15 in May 2015, he became the youngster ever player in Norway's top flight.

ANDRÉ ONANA

The Ajax team of 2018/19 was packed full of exciting young stars from front to back. They won the Eredivisie league title and made it to the Champions League semi-finals, and a decisive member of that journey was goalkeeper André Onana, who made some vital saves in big moments. Still under 25, Onana has stayed at the club while others have left, but it must only be a matter of time before Onana himself moves to one of Europe's biggest clubs. What sets the Cameroon international aside from his peers, as well as his obvious shot-stopping ability, is his comfort with the ball at his feet. Ajax are renowned for coaching players to express themselves on the ball, and Onana is no different.

DID YOU KNOW: Onana's cousin Fabrice Ondoa also plays professional football as a goalkeeper, and the two have featured in the same Cameroon squad.

EWA PAJOR

If you were to try to find the most dangerous strike partnership in world football, VfL Wolfsburg duo Ewa Pajor and Pernille Harder would be in contention. Pajor is the younger player of the two but in 2018/19 she outscored her prolific sidekick by six goals, hitting 24 in league action to Harder's 18 as Wolfsburg won a fifth consecutive title, Pajor's third. The battle to top the scoring charts resumed in 2019/20 with Pajor hitting 12 at the halfway point in all competitions, including two against nearest rivals Bayern Munich. If Pajor continues to learn from her teammate, and score with such regularity and in big games, she could become a powerful force for years to come.

DID YOU KNOW: Pajor was born to score goals. In one season at her first club, Polish side Konin, she netted more than 50 times. For Poland's U17s, she once scored 13 goals in one game.

NIKITA PARRIS

Nikita Parris swapped Manchester City for Olympique Lyonnais in 2019 and though she now faces incredible competition for places in a star-studded squad, she's more than holding her own. She closed 2019 with two goals in her last three games for the French side, a strong ending to a life-changing year in which Parris won a domestic cup double with City – to take her tally of trophies with the club to five – and the SheBelieves Cup with England. Parris ended the 2018/19 Women's Super League (WSL) season with seven assists and 19 goals in 19 games to become the league's all-time top scorer. She was later crowned the Footballer Writer's Association's Women Footballer of the Year.

DID YOU KNOW: Parris did two of her GCSEs – maths and English – while away on England duty. 'Our invigilator would just be one of the coaches,' she told the Daily Telegraph.

MALLORY PUGH

Pugh has been playing at the highest level for what feels like so long you'd be forgiven for thinking that she was older than 22 years of age, but it's pretty clear the wide player has a promising future ahead of her. Capable of scoring goals from either flank and difficult to defend against in one-on-one situations, Pugh impressed on international duty as USA lifted a second consecutive World Cup. She scored in the thrashing of Thailand in the opening match and then featured in every game that followed, including the final. Since then she's been back among the goals for club and country, though it's clear there's plenty more to come at club level.

DID YOU KNOW: In 2015, Pugh was 17 when she became the youngest player for a decade to get a USA call-up. A year later she became the youngest female player to score for USA.

MARCUS RASHFORD

Marcus Rashford is one of the most exciting attacking young talents in world football and in the calendar year of 2019 he scored 25 goals for club and country, eight goals in 13 matches in one particularly hot streak. He started 2020 by making his 200th appearance for United and thereby became the third youngest player to do so, behind Ryan Giggs and George Best. In those 200 games, he scored 64 goals and registered 26 assists. Manchester born and bred and a United supporter as a kid, Rashford excels cutting in from the left side. He looked set for his best ever return in front of goal in 2019/20 having netted 19 goals at the halfway stage.

DID YOU KNOW: Rashford is the only Manchester United player in history to score on his debut in three separate competitions: the Europa League, Premier League and EFL Cup.

ANDREW ROBERTSON

Full-back Andrew Robertson is perfect proof that hard work pays off. The Scot was rejected by Celtic aged 15 and had to work part-time to supplement his earnings at his next club, Queens Park. Now, though, he's considered one of the best left-backs in the world. So, how did he do it? His rise started at Dundee United, with whom he won the PFA Scotland Young Player of the Year award. He moved to Hull City, then Liverpool in 2017. He had to wait until December that year to earn his starting place, but in 2018/19 he was incredible. He won the Champions League, was named in the PFA Team of the Year, and was awarded the Scotland captaincy.

DID YOU KNOW: In 2018/19, Robertson's pinpoint crossing ability from left-back saw him contribute 13 assists in all competitions for Liverpool.

JADON SANCHO

Jadon Sancho must be the most talked-about player when it comes to transfer gossip. It seems that every top club in Europe wants to sign the tricky winger, who's now considered one of the continent's most talented attacking players. Inexperienced when he swapped Manchester City for Borussia Dortmund in 2018, Sancho has been able to flourish with the more game time he's given. He scored 12 goals and a league-high 14 assists in his first season and become only the fourth teenager in history to score 20 goals or more in the Bundesliga during his second. Such form has seen him called up to the England senior side.

DID YOU KNOW: Sancho has averaged a goal or an assist in every other game overall in his 18-month spell in Germany. By February 2020 he'd scored or assisted 45 goals in 64 games.

KHADIJA SHAW

Young Jamaican star Shaw enjoyed a breakout year in 2019. Long touted as a player with potential, and after being named the Guardian Footballer of the Year in 2018, she showed her class on the biggest stage when she led Jamaica – the first Caribbean side to qualify for a women's World Cup – in France in 2019. And while she couldn't replicate her pre-tournament form, in which she scored four goals in two games, against Chile and Scotland, or help her side qualify from the group, she has since continued her fine form at French side Bordeaux. She netted twice on her debut and again in her second game. By Christmas, she had seven goals and five assists.

> DID YOU KNOW: Shaw continues to use personal tragedy to drive her career; she has lost four of seven brothers and two nephews.

DONNY VAN DE BEEK

Another member of the Ajax squad who rose to prominence in 2018/19 by winning the club a 34th league title and reaching the Champions League semi-finals, van de Beek is a classy midfielder who makes the game look easy but who also packs a powerful punch in the final third. He can link play, deliver a defence-splitting pass and make dangerous runs between the lines and into the box. He's also ludicrously comfortable with the ball at his feet, even when under pressure or in tight situations. Such was van de Beek's influence during 2018/19 that he was listed on the 30-man shortlist for the Ballon d'Or.

> DID YOU KNOW: In his first full season at Ajax, in 2017/18, van de Beek scored his first hat-trick and finished the campaign with 13 goals. Not a bad start!

HAKIM ZIYECH

Like so many of his teammates, Ziyech was already doing brilliant things with a football at his feet before Ajax's glorious 2018/19 campaign broadcast his talents to a bigger audience. Ziyech was a key attacking component of the team in that season, scoring 21 goals and adding 18 assists while also pressing opposing wide players at the other end of the pitch. And far from struggle since the subsequent sale of some of his teammates, Ziyech has continued to play to a very high standard; he'd scored eight goals and registered 21 assists by the midway point of the 2019/20 season, enough to secure a move to Chelsea.

DID YOU KNOW: In the 2010s, Ziyech scored 31 goals from outside the 18-yard box and contributed 87 assists, more than any other player in the Dutch Eredivisie.

THE NEARLY LIST!

Tammy Abraham
David Alaba
Dele Alli
Dani Alves
Pierre-Emerick
  Aubameyang
Kepa Arrizabalaga
Arthur
Sergio Busquets
Casemiro
Edinson Cavani
Philippe Coutinho
Cristiane
Alphonso Davies
Ángel di María
Bruno Fernandes

David de Gea
Gianluigi
  Donnarumma
Paulo Dybala
Christian Eriksen
Nilla Fischer
Phil Foden
Antoine Griezmann
Álex Grimaldo
Mattéo Guendouzi
Samir Handanović
Jordan Henderson
Lucas Hernandez
Mauro Icardi
Ciro Immobile
Gabriel Jesus

Vinícius Júnior
Lee Kang-in
Ibrahima Konaté
Kalidou Koulibaly
Toni Kroos
Alexandre Lacazette
Alban Lafont
Kim Little
Gabriel Martinelli
Donyell Malen
Dries Mertens
Marquinhos
Marta
Luke Modrić
Mason Mount
David Neres
Alexander Nübel
Paul Pogba

Sergio Ramos
Rodri
Rodrygo
Bukayo Saka
Leroy Sané
David Silva
Milan Škriniar
Luis Suárez
Dominik Szoboszlai
Dušan Tadić
Ferran Torres
Jamie Vardy
Raphaël Varane
Marco Verratti
Aaron Wan-Bissaka
Timo Werner
Georginio Wijnaldum
Duván Zapata

FOOTBALL STARS
FANTASY XI

Now it's time for you to choose who you think makes the starting XI. Choose players from the list on the right to create your own dream team.

THE DREAM TEAM SHEET

Aergio Agüero

Trent Alexander-Arnold

Alisson Becker

Karim Benzema

Aitana Bonmati

Lucy Bronze

Kevin De Bruyne

Ellie Carpenter

Sara Däbritz

Debinha

Matthijs de Ligt

Frenkie de Jong

Crystal Dunn

Ederson

Christiane Endler

Julie Ertz

Fabinho

João Félix

Fernandinho

Roberto Firmino

Serge Gnabry

Caroline Graham Hansen

Jackie Groenen

Erling Braut Haaland

Achraf Hakimi

Pernille Harder

Kai Havertz

Eden Hazard

Tobin Heath

Ada Hegerberg

Amandine Henry

Jenni Hermoso

Son Heung-Min

Lindsey Horan

Harry Kane

N'Golo Kanté

Samantha Kerr

Joshua Kimmich

Fran Kirby

Saki Kumagai

Aymeric Laporte

Rose Lavelle

Eugénie Le Sommer

Robert Lewandowski

Amel Majri

Sadio Mané

Lieke Martens

Griedge Mbock Bathy

Beth Mead

Vivianne Miedema

Dzsenifer Marozsán

Alex Morgan

Kylian Mbappé

Lionel Messi

Neymar

Manuel Neuer

Jan Oblak

Martin Ødegaard

André Onana

Ewa Pajor

Nikita Parris

Alex Popp

Mallory Pugh

Megan Rapinoe

Marcus Rashford

Wendie Renard

Andrew Robertson

Cristiano Ronaldo

Mohamed Salah

Jadon Sancho

Khadija Shaw

Bernardo Silva

Raheem Sterling

Marc-André ter Stegen

Donny van de Beek

Virgil van Dijk

Daniëlle van de Donk

Sari van Veenendaal

Ellen White

Hakim Ziyech

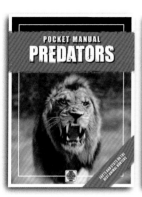

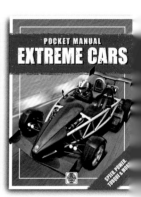